POCKET GUIDE FOR TEENS

Survive Attacks

Land That Date!

Handle Fame (Hey! It Could Happen!)

Make a Million Dollars

D1472808

HONOR **HB** BOOKS

Inspiration and Motivation for the Season of Life

An Imprint of Cook Communications Ministries
COLORADO SPRINGS, COLORADO • PARIS, ONTARIO
KINGSWAY COMMUNICATIONS, LTD., EASTBOURNE, ENGLAND

Honor Books® is an imprint of
Cook Communications Ministries, Colorado Springs, CO 80918
Cook Communications, Paris, Ontario
Kingsway Communications, Eastbourne, England

POCKET GUIDE FOR TEENS
© 2004 by HONOR BOOKS
© 2004 by COOK COMMUNICATIONS MINISTRIES

First printing, 2004
Printed in the UNITED STATES OF AMERICA
2 3 4 5 6 Printing/Year 08 07 06 05 04

Developed by Bordon Books

Written and compiled by Killian Creative, Boulder, Colorado
www.killiancreative.com

ISBN 1-56292-131-2

Contents

Introduction

Ever notice that life seems to come without an instruction manual? We have a few books we look to for the heavy stuff, like we use the Bible to learn how to treat people and to get insight into the nature of our existence. Heavy stuff.

But what about the day-to-day, practical stuff, like how to handle parents, or how to arrange things for the prom? No one ever tells you *how* to pack a suitcase, and don't you just hate sitting in a restaurant and wondering what to do with all the silverware and how much to tip? It is much nicer to be in the know ahead of time.

This is the book to get you where you want to go. Ever wonder about how to get that first job? We've got that covered. Wonder how to arrange your prom date? Yep, it's here. Teachers? Yep. Fame? Yep. (Hey! It could happen! And don't you want to be ready for it?) What about dating? We cover the options like not dating at all, group dates, and your basic, *bona fide* date. Ever wonder how to let someone down easy? That's here too. We'll tell you how to get that date, get that job—we even tell you how to save a million dollars.

Pocket Guide for Teens is sassy, fun with an attitude, and packed with all kinds of practical advice and lists of places where you can get even more advice on the things people forget to tell you and the things they might not know themselves. *(And there's me! I point out the good stuff!)*

Leaf through. The topics are alphabetical so you can easily find them, and there is a detailed table of contents. This is a book you'll want to use every day. We even have places where you can list things and answer questions that will get you moving toward your goal.

You have your whole life before you. Check it out.

GOSSIP ATTACKS (Words are brutal!)

The old saying "Sticks and stones can break your bones, but words will never hurt you" never took into account how badly we can hurt on the inside when vicious things are said about us. *(You got that right!)* While it is true that such words don't leave any permanent physical scars, it is up to us to make sure that they don't leave any permanent psychological scars either.

Here are some things that you can do to make sure that your heart stays clean through it all:

Forgive. Before you do anything else, clear your heart before God and forgive those who have spoken wickedly about you. The Bible tells us repeatedly that unforgiveness does us more harm than the person who hurt us.

Don't feed the fire. Proverbs 26:20 NLT tells us, *Fire goes out for lack of fuel, and quarrels disappear when gossip stops.* Don't counterattack. If people don't see you publicly lash back or overreact, then it often kills the fun of gossiping about you and it will stop. As much as you can, don't fuel their gossiping with more things to say about you.

Talk it out face-to-face. As the old saying goes, "Honesty is the best policy." If you have been hurt by someone, then go speak with them one-on-one and tell them how what they said hurt you. Let them know that you have forgiven them. If they still are spiteful, then it is no longer your problem. You have done what you should and they need to deal with their own problems. But more often you will win back a friend.

Gossip can be like a time bomb *(Yow!)*: If you ignore it or pretend like it isn't there, it will eventually explode; but if you defuse it, it can harmlessly be thrown away. Choose to defuse, not explode.

IF YOU DON'T LIKE OTHERS GOSSIPING ABOUT YOU, DON'T GOSSIP ABOUT OTHERS

Gossip tends to be a two-way street that can quickly turn into a four-lane interstate highway if you aren't careful. Be honest, it is fun to talk about others, especially if you are making yourself look better in the process. *(You are getting personal there!)* Anytime you say something bad about someone else, then it is as if you are lifting yourself up a little in the eyes of those you tell. The problem is that this works only in the short run. In the long run, you are just setting yourself up for a fall. As the old saying goes, "What goes around comes around." Whatever gossip you plant out there about others will eventually come back to you even worse. But if you don't sow seeds of gossip, you won't reap that harvest.

What you do want is a harvest of respect and friendship. So, if you are going to say anything about others, say things that make them look better in the eyes of your friends. Don't do it in a way that cuts yourself down either. It is also a temptation to make fun of ourselves to make others look better because of our own insecurities—in fact, that is the same reason most people gossip, because they are insecure themselves. *(Ouch!)* But don't play the insecurity game on the tearing-down side; play it on the building-up side. If you make others feel better about themselves, they will want to do the same for you.

Sure, you will still feel insecure from time to time *(Hey, insecurity is my middle name, too!)*. That is normal for everyone—but it doesn't help to tear down others or yourself because of it. That will only make you feel even lower in the long run. The key is to reverse the trend—if you want a harvest of nice things said about you, then plant nice things said about others.

 THINK TWICE

If you don't have anything good to say, don't say anything at all.
ANONYMOUS

(It's going to be awfully quiet around here, Mr. Anonymous!)

SOMETHING GOD HAS PROMISED YOU

Keep a clear conscience before God so that when people throw mud at you, none of it will stick. They'll end up realizing that they're the ones who need a bath. 1 PETER 3:16 THE MESSAGE

WARM FUZZIES AND COLD PRICKLIES

Once upon a time, people in a certain tiny village were very happy because they received a bag of Warm Fuzzies at birth. Other people on the street, at home, everywhere received Warm Fuzzies. Warm Fuzzies made you feel just like they sound—warm, happy, and contented. So, everyone in the village was pretty happy all the time—everyone, that is, except the grump at the end of the lane.

Now he had a bag of Warm Fuzzies too, but he ignored it, and by doing that for so long he made himself miserable. Then seeing everyone else happy made him even grumpier. So he went to a neighboring town over the mountains and came back with a bag of Cold Pricklies. They grew incredibly well in the foul soil behind his house. Soon he had tons of them.

So one day he took a bag into the street and waited for someone to give him a Warm Fuzzy. "Thank you very much," he said, "but are you sure that you have enough to spare?" "What do you mean?" the boy asked. "Well," he replied, "if you keep giving away all of your Warm Fuzzies, eventually you will run out. Here, take a bag of these and give them out instead, so you can keep the others."

At first the boy didn't use the bag, but he wasn't giving out as many Warm Fuzzies either. Soon he gave out his first Cold Prickly. It made him feel smarter and more important than those so blindly giving away their Warm Fuzzies. Others began to get concerned about their supply of Warm Fuzzies. The grump was passing out bags of Cold Pricklies by the dozens.

To save their Warm Fuzzies, the whole village started giving away only Cold Pricklies. Everyone was gloomy and very grouchy. Before long there wasn't a Warm Fuzzy to be found anywhere in town. The funny thing was that the grump still didn't feel any better, but at least everyone else was as miserable as he was now!

(Hmmm, . . . I felt better before I read this!)

GETTING GOD INVOLVED

If you have been in a situation where others have been talking hurtfully about you, stop and think before you strike back. *(Or better yet, instead of striking back.)*

Sit and listen to your heart. Have there been others whom you have said hurtful things about? List them here and what you said.

1. _____

2. _____

3. _____

Now, take a minute to pray and ask for forgiveness concerning these. If you are unsure how to pray, you can use the prayer below or make up one of your own.

Father, Please forgive me for the things that I have said about others that may have hurt them. Please take the bad feelings out of my heart that created these words I said and replace them with Your love. Put a doorkeeper on my mouth so that I will realize in the future that I am starting to say such things and help me to stop before I have hurt someone again. From now on help my words to reflect Your love and not my own insecurities. Amen

PUT YOUR ZZZ MIND AT REST

What you feel inside of you determines what you say out of your mouth. If you will keep yourself clean before God on the inside, then the things that come out of your mouth won't fuel hurt and insecurity in both yourself and others.

OVERCOMING OBSTACLES

List some situations that cause hurtful things to be said and come up with some ways to change these bad things into something good. *Example:*

OBSTACLE: My friends and I gossip at lunch.

POSSIBLE SOLUTIONS: I am going to share the Warm Fuzzie and Cold Prickles story with them next time we get together and start a conversation about how I have been hurt by what others have said about me. Next I am going to tell them I don't want to be a part of gossip anymore because it hurts people so badly, and then I'm going to see what they have to say. *(Moan! Then it may be me and Jesus for lunch alone forever!)*

OBSTACLE:

_____

POSSIBLE SOLUTIONS:

_____

_____

OBSTACLE:

_____

POSSIBLE SOLUTIONS:

_____

_____

THE MAIN THING

A FIRE CAN'T BURN WITHOUT FUEL; CUT GOSSIP OFF AT ITS SOURCE—DON'T LET IT COME OUT OF YOUR MOUTH AND TELL OTHERS YOU DON'T WANT TO HEAR IT IF THEY START.

DRIVE-BY AND SCHOOL SHOOTINGS/TERRORISM

School shootings and gang violence have never been more of a cause for concern than they are today, and since September 11, 2001, it seems that no place is safe from such potential attacks any more. It used to be that drive-by shootings were confined only to large cities, but with kids taking guns to school in places such as Pearl, Mississippi; Jonesboro, Arkansas; Springfield, Oregon; or at Columbine school in Littleton, Colorado, there is no longer any-place that seems safe. *(Buy your flak-jackets here, folks!)*

Yet the greatest enemy is not the people who commit these attacks, but *the fear that they provoke.* Sure, we should still be vigilant and careful, but when we face things in fear rather than in faith that God is with us through whatever happens, we do harm to our lives whether we ever face one of these random acts of violence or not. If we continually make our decisions on what *"might someday, maybe, happen,"* then those who want to terrorize us will have already won. If we get to the point that we are afraid to do certain things because we are afraid of what might happen if we do, then we are handi-capping ourselves.

Though the danger is real, it is better to face life in faith that we can be part of the solution rather than in fear that something horrible is bound to happen to us someday. In many ways, fear is part of the process that has caused such things in the first place—those who commit such acts of violence are frustrated and afraid of others, so they seek to destroy things and people senselessly and irrationally. We have to overcome fear before we can do anything else. Then we can have the courage to reach out to others in a way that might just keep someone from committing such attacks. *(Can I still keep my bulletproof undies?)*

💭 THINK TWICE

There is nothing to fear but fear itself.

FRANKLIN DELANO ROOSEVELT

SOMETHING GOD HAS PROMISED **YOU**

(OR GOD IS BETTER THAN A BULLETPROOF VEST! YEAH!)

For God has said, "I will never fail you. I will never forsake you."

*That is why we can say with confidence,
"The Lord is my helper, so I will not be afraid.
What can mere mortals do to me?"* HEBREWS 13:5-6 NLT

GETTING DOWN TO THE

Prevent. Overcoming fear is just the first thing that we need to do though. The next is to try to be a positive force to prevent such things from happening in the first place. How can we do that? One way is to be a factor in our own communities for connecting people with one another rather than allowing people to "disconnect" in ways that lead to violence and other self-destructive behaviors. Gang violence erupts because kids have no better group to connect with in their neighborhoods than the gangs that offer them protection and friendship in exchange for their loyalty and allegiance; school shootings seem to happen when kids are disconnected from people at school or have no better expression for their feelings than striking out violently at others; terrorism happens because our world has allowed itself to be divided into haves and have-nots, with one group dominating the other group until they strike back in frustration and anger. As Jesus said, "Every kingdom divided against itself will be ruined" (Matthew 12:25). We can keep alert to those in need and learn to recognize the danger signs of others who are disconnecting in frustration. The other person may not be ready to attack someone, but it is still good to reach out to others and help when you can. So be a friend and make the world a safer place.

Protect. There are things that you can do to protect yourself as well. Learning basic self-defense or how to negotiate with people may never be used in a life-and-death situation and may not defend against a bullet, but it will help you take the edge off fear and give you more confidence in other areas of your life. Talk with your teachers and principal to see what emergency plans are in place and help in any way that you can. *(TWEEET! All right, everybody! Quit hiding in the dumpster!)* Make sure that others are informed as well. Take a basic first aid and CPR course. It is amazing how little it can take to save a life in a critical situation. Often the only difference between a hero and a bystander is having the courage and knowledge to act.

MAKE A DIFFERENCE BY DOING SOME OF THESE

↳ Remember to pray for God's protection on your leaders, your nation, and your community.

↳ Attend a city council meeting or find out what is being done in your community to stop violent crimes. See how you can help.

↳ Start a discussion group at your school to address the issues of violence and fear.

↳ Talk with your family and be sure you have an emergency plan at home in case of fire, break-ins, etc. *(Acne break outs . . . Hey! This can be an emergency sometimes!)*

↳ Be an example of God's love wherever you go.

HELPFUL WEB SITES

Find your local chapter of the Red Cross and sign up for First Aid/CPR training, find out about donating blood, or volunteering. www.redcross.org

The U. S. Department of Homeland Security's Web site is www.ready.gov

HELPFUL BOOKS

Prayers that Avail Much for Teens by Germaine Copeland (Harrison House, 2003)

The Worst-Case Scenario Survival Handbook by Joshua Piven and David Borgenicht (Chronicle Books: 1999)

FEAR BUSTERS

Keep things in perspective. Though violence and attacks are very real in our times, as a whole the odds are in our favor that we will not be attacked. Don't let fear blow things out of proportion. Do what is smart in order to be informed and also take precautions, but don't get carried away with it. *(Honest, Teacher, I would've done my homework, but I had to save the world last weekend!)*

Count your blessings. Look at all of the good around you for a moment. Overall, most of us have pretty good lives, and we need to be grateful for that.

Support your local heroes. Recognize that there are people around you who are willing to risk their lives for yours every day: firemen, police officers, and other emergency workers. At your school, church, or through some other organization do something to show your appreciation for them. Learn from them what you can do to help keep your community safe and secure.

 FEAR STOMPING WORDS

Where God's love is, there is no fear, because God's perfect love drives out fear. 1 JOHN 4:18 NCV

Faith liberates.
Fear incapacitates.

DC TALK
JESUS FREAKS 2

KICK IT IN GEAR

List five things that you can do to defeat fear, prevent violence, and protect your family, friends, and classmates.

1. _____

2. _____

3. _____

4. _____

5. _____

(Hey, how come you didn't fill in the blanks! C'mon, you can think of some things!)

THE MAIN THING

TRUSTING IN GOD AND BEING AFRAID ARE LIKE LIGHT AND DARKNESS: WHEN THE FIRST IS TURNED ON, THE OTHER FLEES.

CLIQUES AND CLUBS— HOW TO BREAK INTO A GROUP

MAKING FRIENDS AND BEATING THE_CLIQUE_BARRIER

It is tough feeling left out. When you see a group of people talking in the hall and one of them catches your eye momentarily and then looks back to the other without saying "Hi," or even registering that they saw you, it can really hurt! Why do people have to be so cliquish? *(Yeah, that hurts. So how can I get my eye back?)*

Well, first of all, people tend to be drawn towards other people who are like they are. Some may be openly rude in excluding others, but they are the exception. Most people just hang out with others who have similar interests and don't understand those who don't. So football players hang out with football players, cheerleaders with other cheerleaders, and the kids in the computer club with other kids who like computers. Not all of that is bad. It is simply a way of finding acceptance from others and learning for the first time to be a part of a group other than your immediate family. It is part of growing up and becoming functioning social beings.

The problem, of course, is when those interest groups become exclusive and shut others out or even make fun of those who are not in their "in" group. How do you fit in when you are definitely different from the group you want to fit in with?

First of all, don't sell yourself short. Just because you are different from others in a group doesn't mean that you are somehow inferior—in fact, it often means the opposite. *(Well, of course! Duh!)* If a group is so narrow-minded that they don't see the value of others, then they definitely have some growing up to do. And don't try to change who you are just to fit in. Be yourself no matter what—after all, God created you as you!

Yet on the other hand, don't be so stuck on who you are that you can't be open-minded, or become different just to be noticed. Otherwise you are just as stuck-up and narrow-minded in rejecting popular kids as they are to you. All you do is add more barriers.

So what do you do? Here are some simple starters:

1. **Be sincerely interested in others.** It is amazing how well you can be liked if you don't do most of the talking! Ask others about themselves and then just listen. Learn to "interview" people about their interests and what they like, and they will be glad to talk to you for a long time. Then watch the tide turn—if you ask questions about others, then they will ask questions about you. That is where the chance to make a friend really begins. *(All right! Social life, here I come!)*

2. **Follow the Golden Rule: Treat others the same way that you would want them to treat you.** Courtesy is always appreciated, even if it is not shown toward you. Many people get the Golden Rule backwards. They think it is "Treat others the same way they have treated you." Or in other words, be nice to those who are nice and rude to those who are rude. But that is not how it works. Regardless of how people act, you act towards them as you would want them to act towards you. This is the kindness that breaks down barriers.

3. **Join. Sign up. Try out.** There is really nothing wrong with being an athlete, a cheerleader, a student council member, or becoming a member of whatever group you would like to be a part of. But if you like those things and want to be part of them, then you should sign up to join. *(Why not go for it!)* Run for class vice president or try out for the baseball team. If you don't try, you can't join! Now you may not make it, but so what? At least you gave it a shot and you will have made some new friends by just going through the process—and after all, isn't that what we are talking about here?

 THINK TWICE *(AND MORE OFTEN IF NECESSARY!)*

Blessed are they who have the gift of making friends,
for it is one of God's best gifts. It involves many things,
but above all, the power of going out of one's self, and
appreciating whatever is noble and loving in another.

THOMAS HUGHES

SOMETHING GOD HAS PROMISED YOU

There are "friends" who destroy each other, but a real friend
sticks closer than a brother. PROVERBS 18:24 NLT

MAKE FRIENDS BY REMEMBERING THIS

↳ If you like yourself, then it will be easier for others to like you as well.

↳ You will become better at the things you invest more time in: read, practice, or do the other things that you like to do.

↳ Call others who enjoy doing the things you like, and don't wait around for someone to call you when you are bored. *(Right! There's no 1-800-BOREDOM!)*

↳ Pick up a new hobby that interests you: learn to play the guitar, learn to draw better, or design your own clothes and then make them. If you develop new interests, you will create new ways for others to connect with you.

↳ Find a summer job where other teens work.

↳ Always remember to be the best person you can be.

HELPFUL BOOKS

How To Win Friends and Influence People by Dale Carnegie (Pocket Books, 1990)

How to Start a Conversation and Make Friends: Revised and Updated by Don Gabor (Fireside, 2001)

OVERCOMING OBSTACLES

List the things you think will slow you down. *(Hmmm ... Making lists of obstacles slows me down!) Example:*

OBSTACLE: I want to be a cheerleader, but I don't have the steps.

POSSIBLE SOLUTIONS: I will take some dance lessons and do whatever else I can so that next fall I can make the team. I may not be the prettiest, but I will learn to be enthusiastic and have a big smile all of the time, because that is what cheerleading is really about.

OBSTACLE _____

POSSIBLE SOLUTIONS: _____

_____

OBSTACLE _____

POSSIBLE SOLUTIONS: _____

_____

PUT YOUR 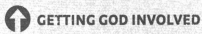 MIND AT REST

Breaking into a new group is not about being more popular; it is about doing the things that you like to do and being with others who share your interests.

GETTING GOD INVOLVED

Talk to God about making new friends and breaking into new groups.

Sit for a while and listen. Write down anything He brings to mind.

1. _____

2. _____

3. _____

4. _____

5. _____

Now take a minute to pray about these. You can use the prayer below or make up one of your own.

Father, Help me to be more friendly and interested in others. Help me to ask the right questions when I meet new people and that will help me learn more about them and find out what really makes them tick. Please also lead me to friends who will be true friends, and give me the ability to tell the difference between those who can be real friends and those who would be false friends. Thank You as well for helping me to break through barriers and make friends who will make me a better person. Amen

THE MAIN THING

TO MAKE FRIENDS, BE A FRIEND.

(I've always wondered . . . if Barbie is so popular, why do we have to buy her friends?)

FRIENDLY FIRE

(What's up with that "peer" thing?)

One of the downsides to being in a group is that sometimes they can pressure you to do things that you know you shouldn't. That can be pretty tough to handle, especially if they are older and you are trying to fit in. What do you do when they pressure you to do something you know is wrong? Is it such a big thing that you might risk losing your friends over it? Do you wonder, if you go along just this once, *maybe it won't be that big of a deal?* (Hmmm ... tough call.)

Before you respond, maybe you should first realize that God didn't design friends to pressure you to do things that you think are wrong, but to encourage you to do what is right. Peer pressure isn't actually supposed to be a negative thing, but a positive thing to build you up. A good peer group will encourage you to get out from in front of the TV and go ride bikes, go to the mall, work on a community service project with them, or some other positive thing. They may be getting you to do things that you aren't comfortable with, but at least they are good things. If your friends are encouraging you to do things that are wrong, then perhaps you should evaluate whether or not they are *really* friends.

Another thing is that friends can take a "No" from you and still be friends. (New slogan: Just Say No to friends!) If you are always doing only what they want to do, then you are not their friend, but just part of their entourage, just there to make them look good. True friends can handle differences of opinions or likes and dislikes.

And also, it may be hard to get you to compromise your values the first time, but once that barrier is broken, then it is easier and easier to get you to agree to do things that may be worse.

So put yourself and your "friends" to the test. Say "No" when you should. Then you will see whether they are your friends or not.

 THINK TWICE

My best friend is the one who brings out the best in me.

HENRY FORD

To get nowhere, follow the crowd.

CHARLIE BROWN

SOMETHING GOD HAS PROMISED YOU

You use steel to sharpen steel, and one friend sharpens another.

PROVERBS 27:17 THE MESSAGE

STICKING TO HER CONVICTIONS

Chelsea stood with her friends in line at the multiplex chattering and giggling. It was the first night of summer vacation and Chelsea was going to be a freshman next year. She was so excited when one of the guys from the youth group called and asked her to go to the movies with him and a group of friends.

When they got to the front of the line, however, her excited chatter stopped when she saw the boy who had called her go up and order tickets for an R-rated horror movie. "C,mon, Brad, don't kid," she said, trying to keep her smile. "We're not going to see that movie—it's way too gross." She didn't add what was really on her mind though: She wasn't allowed to see R-rated films.

"Oh, c'mon yourself!" Brad replied snidely. "What did you think we were going to go see, some kiddie film? Grow up! You're in high school now. Besides, you can sit by me; I'll keep you safe." The others laughed.

Chelsea didn't like something in the way he said that last thing. A chill ran down her spine. "I'm sorry, I can't." The others egged her on and called her names, but she just turned on her heels and walked away with the tears starting in the corners of her eyes. She saw a pay phone across the way and headed for it. She felt so alone, and the pay phone seemed so far away.

When she got there she fumbled with her purse for a moment as the tears came more steadily. *I thought they wanted me to be their friend,* she thought. *What do they really want with me?*

"Hey, Chelsea, wait!" Chelsea wiped her eyes quickly and looked up to see Lauren coming towards her, alone. "Thanks for doing that," she said. "I didn't know what to do. My parents don't let me see R-rated films either. Want to go see something else?"

Chelsea smiled, relieved, and nodded. Maybe things would work out okay.

KICK IT IN GEAR

List some things here that you have felt pressured to do, know that you shouldn't do, and also know you have the strength to resist.

1. _____

2. _____

3. _____

Pray over these things so that God will keep you strong in doing right.

WANT TO LEARN TO HANDLE PEER PRESSURE?
TRY THESE SOURCES!

Life Strategies for Teens by Jay McGraw (Fireside, 2000)

When People Are Big and God Is Small: Overcoming Peer Pressure, Codependency, and the Fear of Man (Resources for Changing Lives) by Edward T. Welch (P & R Press, 1997)

THE MAIN THING

A FRIEND WHO DOESN'T ENCOURAGE YOU TO BECOME A BETTER PERSON IS NOT A FRIEND.

(One who encourages you to become a bitter person isn't a friend, either!)

HOW TO BE PART OF THE TEAM

Michael Jordan dribbles the ball over the centerline with eight seconds left on the clock. The Chicago Bulls trail by a point. He makes a move and looks to have a clear shot at the top of the key—but passes to Scotty Pippen under the basket for an easy layup instead. The final buzzer sounds—the Bulls win again!

While Michael Jordon has been recognized time and again by many people as the greatest athlete of our time and the greatest basketball player of all time, what most people don't realize is that one of his greatest skills was his passing ability and his instinct for when to dish off a ball to one of his teammates and when to take the shot himself—in other words, his ability to be a team player. Michael, and all other great athletes as well, knew that teamwork was the key to victory, not his individual stardom.

It has long been said that there is no "I" in the word "team" *(I can't spell, but even I knew THAT!)*—and this is true whether it is a sports team, a cheerleading team, a team working together to produce a yearbook or school newspaper, a team put together to give a presentation in history, a youth group, or even a family. Any group working together to accomplish a common goal is a team, and good teams are those where everyone contributes their best to making that goal happen.

When one person hogs the spotlight over all the others, feelings get hurt and suddenly no one has their best to contribute anymore. So true team players work not only to give their best, but also work to ensure that others can as well. They build up those who are having a tough time, encourage each other, and make sure that the credit is shared equally.

If you want to be part of a team, first be sure that you are willing to be a team player.

GETTING DOWN TO THE NITTY GRITTY

Here are three main keys that you need to do in order to become a team player:

1. **Communicate.** Communication is the oil that lubricates the gears of a team. Without it the gears don't join together properly or they chafe one another. When everyone knows what is going on and what the other team members need, it is easier to work together. It is also important to know when someone is under a heavy workload and needs help as much as when someone feels that they are not getting the credit they deserve or are feeling left out.

2. **Have a common vision.** While it may seem obvious what a team's goal is—a sporting team wants to win their games, a yearbook team wants to produce a good yearbook, and a youth group wants to get all of its members closer to Jesus—the how and why of this are not always as clear. If everyone gets involved in these hows and whys, the team comes together more effectively to accomplish their goal. Then you can just do it!

3. **Motivate and encourage one another.** There is an old saying that "A chain is only as strong as its weakest link." *(And I don't want to be the that link!)* This can be true of a team as well. If all of the team members do well, but one fails to do their assignment, then the entire team is let down; or if everything is done well by everyone, but one task in the process is overlooked, then again the team's efforts are for nothing. Because of this, no team member or task can be seen as insignificant. You can't afford to just go in, do your part well, and then take off.

Encourage and help each other when needed so that in the end the entire team wins.

THINK TWICE

It is amazing what you can accomplish if you do not care who gets the credit.

HARRY S TRUMAN *(is "credited" with this saying. Hmmm . . .)*

There is no indispensable man.

FRANKLIN DELANO ROOSEVELT

SOMETHING GOD HAS PROMISED

Under his [Jesus'] direction, the whole body is fitted together perfectly. As each part does its own special work, it helps the other parts grow, so that the whole body is healthy and growing and full of love.

EPHESIANS 4:16 NLT *[insert added]*

THE DEADLINE

Amy was a wiz at writing but also loved playing softball, though her inability to handle pop-ups had kept her benched for most of last season. Because of her combined loves, she wanted to be the sports editor for the school newspaper, but the job went to Ken—a star football and baseball player—because he was a year older and such a jock. Amy got to work on the editorials and interviews, which was also fun, but she could never quite forgive Ken.

So it was hard for Amy not to smirk a bit when she dropped off her stories for the next week's edition of the paper and saw Ken staring blankly at a computer screen in the corner of the newspaper room. Amy crossed to Ken, thinking she would gloat a bit and then leave, but when Ken saw her, a glint of hope flashed in his eyes. "Amy! Great! You are just the person I need! This article is horrible, and I don't have the names of five of the players on the volleyball team. I wish I could make these games sound as exciting as you made the new tree in front of the science lab sound last week! Could you help me out a bit?"

Amy flushed at the praise and forgot her anger at Ken for the moment. Besides, if she showed she could write good sports articles, maybe she could get that beat next year. "Sure," she said. And they sat down to work.

When they had finished about a half hour later, Ken was really thankful. "Amy, you saved my life! That was great!" He thought for a moment, then said, "Hey! Could we make a trade? If you will help me a bit with these articles, maybe I could work with you on your fielding for softball." Amy flushed again at the offer, but didn't hesitate. "I'll bring my mitt tomorrow," she replied.

WANT TO BE A TEAM PLAYER?

The 17 Essential Qualities of a Team Player: Becoming the Kind of Person Every Team Wants by John C. Maxwell (Thomas Nelson, 2002)

FINDING YOUR PLACE ON THE TEAM

Different people have different skills and ways of communicating; recognizing those differences is important to both getting along with and bringing out the best in everyone. While some people are exciters and motivators, they may not be very helpful when the actual work needs to be done because it is hard for them to stay focused on one task for very long. *(Yeah! Now where was I . . . ?)* While others may be diligent, get-things-done workers, they would never want to get up in front of a group—they would rather work on their own. Yet getting these two quite different people together to do a presentation might be incredibly successful. While one makes sure all the details and information are correct, the other is a dynamic presenter in front of the others!

We all have our different styles and our different strengths and weaknesses. While one may get more attention than the other, one is not more important than the other. In sports, newspapers highlight how many touchdowns the tailback scored, but they hardly mention the strong lineman who opened up the holes so that that same tailback was not tackled before he gained a yard! Being a team member means working within your own strengths so that others can work within theirs, thus benefiting the whole team.

Recognizing these differences can also go a long way toward helping a team get along. When you recognize, respect, and even compliment the strengths of others, you make room for your strengths to get noticed as well. And when we let our strengths fill in for others' weaknesses, and vice versa, the whole team becomes stronger as a result.

TEAM-BUILDING WORDS

We confide in our strength, without boasting of it;
we respect that of others without fearing it.

THOMAS JEFFERSON

KICK IT IN GEAR

Pick out one team that you are a member of and list some things you can do to help that team work more effectively.

1. _____

2. _____

3. _____

4. _____

5. _____

THE MAIN THING

BEING A TEAM PLAYER MEANS HELPING EVERY TEAM MEMBER TO CONTRIBUTE THEIR BEST.

FINDING THE BEST SCHOOL FOR YOU

A good thing to realize as you start your search for a good college is that there is no "perfect" school; instead, each college or university is prepared to meet the individual needs of different people. By answering the following questions and starting early in your search, you can narrow your list down to a handful on which to begin your research.

Here are some basic questions that can help you get started though. (For a more detailed list, see some of the resources we have listed later in this section):

1. **What are you interested in studying?** Finding a college that specializes in the field you want to specialize in is a key part of your selection process.

2. **How far away from home are you willing to be?** Are you comfortable with being across the country, or do you want to go home every weekend to do your laundry? *(It could get sticky before the semester is up!)*

3. **How large a school do you want to attend?** Do you get lost in a crowd or do you make a splash in a big pond?

4. **Are you interested in extracurricular opportunities?** *(Besides laundry?)* Are you looking for a great college newspaper to edit or

a winning dance team to join in addition to your regular studies? Or is there some other interest?

Answering these initial questions can do a great job of refining your search from the very beginning. Have fun as you start. It should be a great adventure. *(At least, pretend it's fun!)*

WHAT IF I DON'T KNOW WHAT I WANT TO DO?

There are always those around us who seem to know what they wanted to be from the time they were five—they knew they were headed to medical or law school, they had a knack for drawing that got them interested in graphic arts or architecture, or for some other reason they just knew what they wanted to do and beat a path straight for the schools that would prepare them for those fields and futures. But most of us are not like that. Most of us won't figure out what we want to do until we get into college and have been there for a while. *(Really! Or even later!)* What do we do when we don't have a specific interest, but have several different ones instead?

Well, first of all, you do have help. Many of those around you who are older than high school age have either gone through college or are in college now. Ask for help and have them tell you their stories. The counseling office at your school is there specifically to help you in this process and has a lot of resources—from tests that will line up your interests and skills with which careers would be best for you, to books and study guides to help you study for your SATs or ACTs. Taking advantage of these is a great help in deciding where to go.

Second, if you still have a lot of different interests, then find a college that will help you explore all of those different interests rather than a school that specializes in only one. There are a lot of good liberal arts colleges that will allow you to take courses in all of your areas of interest and even let you switch majors midstream should you change your mind.

If you are unsure what you want to be doing for the rest of your life—unlike your friend who has been beelining for medical school—know that you are not alone in this and that going to college can also be a big part of helping you decide what you will do for the rest of your life, as well as giving you the skills to do it.

THINK TWICE

Apply yourself. Get all the education you can, but then . . . do something. Don't just stand there, make it happen.

LEE IACOCCA

The object of education is to prepare the young to educate themselves throughout their lives.

ROBERT MAYNARD HUTCHINS

(Hmmm . . . that could put my teachers out of a job!)

SOMETHING GOD HAS PROMISED YOU

*Get wisdom! Get understanding!
Do not forget, nor turn away from the words of my mouth.*

*Do not forsake her, and she will preserve you;
Love her, and she will keep you.*

Wisdom is the principal thing; Therefore get wisdom.

PROVERBS 4:5-7 NKJV

HELP FOR FINDING THE RIGHT COLLEGE FOR YOU

↳ Start early and apply early. Many schools have great benefits for their early enrollment candidates. Remember that early bird thing! *(And we all know what worms taste like!)*

↳ Don't apply to only one school. Keep your options open.

↳ Talk with your high school counselor.

↳ Many schools send recruiters to your area. Find out the details from your high school counseling department and go to their meetings. Check the Web sites of schools you are interested in attending and see if they are sending a recruiter your way or if you can contact one online.

HELPFUL WEB SITES

A college/career checklist for middle and high school students http://www.mapping-your-future.org
www.washingtonpost.com/wp-srv/business/longterm/
mym/college/checklst.htm

Many college Web sites can be reached by typing in www.*(type the name of the school)*.edu

If not, go to a standard search engine such as www.google.com and search for the school you are interested in.

College search Web sites
www.collegeboard.com/csearch
www.universities.com/
www.usacolleges.com/
www.FastWeb.com
www.search4careercolleges.com

Information on finding a college, preparing to go, financial aid, and more
www.collegeboard.com
www.collegenet.com

Canadian college search Web site:
www.schoolfinder.com/

For a head-to-head comparison of your favorite schools
www.usnews.com/usnews/edu/college/coworks.htm
(There is a charge for this service.)

To get a better feel for a campus, check out their
college newspaper at http://dir.yahoo.com/News_and_
Media/College_and_University/ Newspapers/

U.S. Department of Education Campus Security Stats
www.ope.ed.gov/security/Search.asp

HELPFUL BOOKS

You're Going to Love This College Guide by Marty Nemko
(Barron's, 1999)

The Princeton Review publishes various guides each year,
many specific to the type of school you are looking for
(Random House)

The Insider's Guide to the Colleges compiled and edited by
the staff of the Yale Daily News (St. Martin's press,
updated each year)

How to Choose a College Major by Linda Landis Andrews
(VGM Career Horizons, 1998)

Check your local bookstores or library for various
books that discuss how to write a college essay or present
samples of successful college essays.

PUT YOUR  MIND AT REST

(zzzzz . . . Oh! Sorry.)

This may seem a huge task, but others have succeeded at it before you. Ask their advice.

🔼 GETTING GOD INVOLVED

Talk to God about what you need from a college and write down anything that He brings to your mind about it.

1. _____

2. _____

3. _____

Now take a minute to pray about these. If you are unsure how to pray, you can use the prayer below or make up one of your own.

Father, Thank You for Your wisdom as I prepare to take this next big step in going to college. Please continue to show me the things I need to be aware of as I go through this process. Guide me to the school that is best for me and help me to know which one it is. Please also help make my time in college a time I can grow closer to You and hear Your voice more clearly. Thank You. Amen

THE MAIN THING 🗝

IT IS THE COLLEGE THAT FITS YOU BEST— NOT THE ONE WITH THE BIGGEST NAME— THAT WILL BE THE BEST FOR YOU.

COLLEGE ON A SHOESTRING

Let's face it: college is expensive, and most of us have not put any money away for it until we are almost ready to go there. Even if you have, then it is still likely you will not have enough to cover all of your expenses. Look at the next section for more about what college really costs. *(Am I sure I want to know this?)* The price of tuition and fees increases on average about five or six percent a year, outpacing the cost of inflation. The only way to beat that is to start now in planning how you will pay for your undergraduate degree. Here are some of the best sources you can tap into to pay for your schooling:

1. **Savings.** Saving money when you are young is still one of the best ways to pay for college. With various college savings plans now available to people who save money on the full price of college—from 529 plans to pre-paid tuition plans—starting early to save is still a must.

2. **Scholarships, grants, and other "free money."** These tend to be extremely competitive, but there are now so many different chances for these, it is crazy not to apply to several. *(Hey! You didn't mention entering the sweepstakes!)*

3. **Working.** Most schools have work-study programs, or you can find a job near campus that doesn't interfere with your class times.

4. **Military programs.** If you are interested in a military career, having them pay for your college is a great first step.

5. **Loans.** Though this is a last option, loans from family members or student institutions go a long way to filling in the cost of college.

Doing the work to go through the application process for these can be a pain, but it will save you a lot of wear and tear in the end if those applications turn into money for your future.

WHAT DOES COLLEGE REALLY COST?

When people sit down to start calculating the cost of college, they often forget there are several other costs to consider to get the total amount. Here are the costs most experts suggest you look at to get the total cost of going to school:

- **Tuition.** This does still tend to be the largest cost to going to school, but people often forget that this increases each year at about five to six percent. So if you are starting your calculations for college as a freshman or younger, make sure you factor in this yearly increase so you know all of what you will owe. See the next section for web calculators to help with this.

- **Fees.** Make sure you also calculate in everything from application fees to lab fees. *(Those white rats aren't cheap and neither are the mazes they run in!)*

- **Room.** This will cost unless you are living at home. This is not just rent, but also utilities, cable, Internet access, etc.

- **Board.** You've got to eat! (And you should learn to cook too!) Learn how to plan meals and budget.

- **Books & Supplies.** This can actually be around $1,000 a year, so be sure to include it.

- **Miscellaneous and Personal Expenses.** You will have to buy your clothes, your movie tickets, and everything else, so include those estimates as well.

- **Transportation.** Getting to and from school costs, whether you drive from home or fly across the country. Figure out the mileage, how many times you will come home a year, and call around to get estimates from different airlines, bus companies, or train services. It is good to calculate the entire wear and tear on your car, not just the gasoline—many companies use 35 cents a mile to calculate such costs.

THINK TWICE

Do not wait; the time will never be "just right." Start where you stand, and work with whatever tools you may have at your command, and better tools will be found as you go along.

NAPOLEON HILL
(Great, great, grandfather of "Tim the Toolman"!)

SOMETHING GOD HAS PROMISED YOU

*Delight yourself in the LORD;
And He will give you the desires of your heart.*

Commit your way to the LORD, Trust also in Him, and He will do it.

PSALM 37:4-5 NASB

WHY START EARLY?

Amount to Save to Have $10,000 When You Begin College
(Assuming a 5 percent interest rate)

Age	Years	Monthly savings	Principal	Interest	Total
Newborn	18	$29	$6,197	$3,803	$10,000
Age 4	14	$41	$6,935	$3,065	$10,000
Age 8	10	$64	$7,736	$2,264	$10,000
Age 12	6	$119	$8,601	$1,399	$10,000
Age 16	2	$397	$9,531	$469	$10,000

(Only $26 if you start early, in the womb!)

HELPFUL 🌐 WEB SITES FOR GETTING FINANCIAL AID

Saving plans to pay for college
www.savingforcollege.com or www.collegesavings.org

Free online scholarship searches:
www.finaid.org
www.FastWeb.com
www.srnexpress.com/index.cfm
www.collegenet.com
www.wiredscholar.com

College Cost/Financial Aid Calculators
www.finaid.org/calculators/
www.studentcollegeloan.com/calculating-cost.html
www.studentloanfunding.com/calcultr/index.html

U.S. Department of Education's Think College site
www.ed.gov/offices/OPE/thinkcollege/welcome/

HELPFUL B👓KS FOR GETTING FINANCIAL AID

The Complete Scholarship Book by FastWeb.com (Sourcebooks, Inc., 2000)

Conquer the Cost of College: Strategies for Financial Aid (Kaplan, 2001)

FEAR BUSTERS

Applying for scholarships and financial aid can be even more scary than applying for college because there is so much more likelihood that you will get rejected. Plus, the forms can be long and tedious or demand essays or other things that you may not be comfortable in producing. *(Essays!? Did you say essays?)* However, just one success can make all the difference in the world.

Ask anyone who has applied for scholarships—they remember the ones they received, but probably not those that they didn't. *(Maybe it's because writing all those essays fried their brains!)*

So be bold and apply for everything that you can think of, and start early in the process so you are not doing everything at the last minute. This will not only lighten the workload, but it will also help you to present better materials that are more likely to get you the money you need to go to school.

FEAR STOMPING WORDS

"With God all things are possible." MARK 10:27 NKJV

Whether you believe you can do a thing or not, you are right.

HENRY FORD
(I believe he's right!)

KICK IT IN GEAR

Name some special skills and interests you have. Then, as you start to look for scholarships or other help, search for programs that are looking for kids with those interests or skills. It may just be that making such a match will be the key to financing your education!

1. _____

2. _____

3. _____

4. _____

THE MAIN THING

THERE ARE A LOT OF OPPORTUNITIES FOR HELP IN PAYING FOR COLLEGE—WORKING TO TAKE ADVANTAGE OF THEM BEFORE AND WHILE YOU ARE IN SCHOOL IS BETTER THAN TAKING YEARS TO PAY OFF COLLEGE LOANS LATER.

COMMUNICATION—VIBES AND ELECTRO-VIBES

PARTY TALK *(Oh, no! What do I say?)*

This weekend you are going to your cousin's birthday party across town and you don't know anyone else from her school. Or maybe you've been invited to a dance at a school you don't attend, or out with a group from your own school, but you hardly know any of them. What are you going to do? You are going to spend the next few hours with these people—how are you going to survive? *(Run!)*

The nice thing about conversations is that they follow a fairly predictable pattern. If you flow with and follow the currents, then you can meet new people, get to know them, and even leave with them liking you, if you just remember one rule: *be more interested in hearing about them than telling them about you.* Too many people think that the key to good conversations is talking, but they are wrong. *The key to good conversations is listening.*

Start with small talk. Most conversation starts with small talk about things everyone knows about: "Boy, today was a hot one, eh?" "What school do you go to?" "What is your favorite subject in school?" Yes, that's right. Little questions anyone can comment on. The problem is that a lot of people get stuck on where to go from there. The key to overcoming that is to realize that small talk is a fishing trip—you are not just talking to pass the time, but to find out what interests you have in common. That is when the real conversations start!

Once you have hit on something you have in common, don't make the mistake of bombarding the other person with all you know; rather, use your knowledge to ask questions and find out what they know about it. Ask "why" questions: ones that can't be answered with a simple yes or no and listen and smile and nod. *(Uh-huh . . . Uh-huh.)* When the conversation lags, ask another question. Make others feel included, comfortable, and important. Follow the flow and you might even learn something new!

Introduce yourself. Once the ice has been broken and you feel more comfortable, introduce yourself. When everyone is on a first-name basis, they will feel more comfortable in the conversation. Many experts say that if you use the other person's name six times in the conversation when you first are introduced, you are more likely to remember their name later. You also make them feel important because you have remembered their name. Don't be phony in this—that can be a real turnoff—but do it sincerely and you may be able to get the conversation to go even deeper.

Real conversation is the goal, but don't force it. There is most definitely a point where conversation turns a corner and more personal and meaningful things can be shared. This is the type of dialogue that friends have after they have known each other for some time and begin to let the other person really begin to see what is in their hearts. This is also something that is pretty rare in our culture. The deeper a conversation is, the more likely you are to have a difference of opinion that can turn into an argument or make the other person feel alienated, so as a rule most people avoid deep conversation in our diverse society. It is also something that is pretty unlikely when first meeting someone. However, from time to time it can develop on its own if given the space and time. Then you may well be on your way to making a new friend.

Sure, this may take some time to master, and you will probably crash and burn a few times because a lot of people are so self-conscious that they are too nervous to talk with someone new. (Just like you were before you read this!) But one nice thing about a party is that there is always someone else to talk to! So give it a try. Before the end of the evening you may well be a master at it; and you will probably have a few new friends as well!

 THINK TWICE

You can make more friends in two months by becoming interested in other people than you can in two years by trying to get other people interested in you.

DALE CARNEGIE

SOMETHING GOD HAS PROMISED YOU

Be gracious in your speech. The goal is to bring out the best in others in a conversation, not put them down, not cut them out.

COLOSSIANS 4:6 THE MESSAGE

QUESTIONS THAT LEAD FROM SMALL TALK TO REAL CONVERSATION

↳ If you could be anyone in the world, who would you be? Why?

↳ What is your favorite book or movie? Why?

↳ Wow, that is a nice name. Why did your parents choose this particular name? Is there a story behind it?

↳ When you get a free day, what do you like to do? Why?

↳ What would you do if someone gave you a million dollars?

↳ Tell me something that no one would ever guess about you.

↳ What is the favorite place that you have ever visited? Why? Would you live there if you could?

↳ I like that shirt (blouse, skirt, shorts, whatever). Where did you get it?

FOR MORE ADVICE ON TALKING WITH OTHERS

How to Start a Conversation and Make Friends: Revised and Updated by Don Gabor (Fireside, 2001)

Conversationally Speaking: Tested New Ways to Increase Your Personal and Social Effectiveness by Alan Garner (McGraw-Hill/Contemporary Books; 1997)

THE MAIN THING

A GOOD LISTENER NEVER HAS ANY SHORTAGE OF FRIENDS.

WRITE OFFICIAL LETTERS AND MAKE OFFICIAL PHONE CALLS

LOOK AND SOUND GOOD IN PRINT

Actually putting your thoughts in writing on paper and then sending a copy of that to someone is still the best way of saying "I want you to know this and have a paper record of it so that you will remember it." What you say in such letters needs to leave them with a good, lasting impression that will encourage them to act on what you have said. Here are some key things to remember:

1. **Put it into print.** With computers and word processing programs available to us today, there is no excuse for handwriting an official letter. Most programs have spelling, grammar, and style checks to help you sound better, as well as templates to help you set up your letter easily. If you want to make a further good impression, use your computer to address the envelope as well.

2. **Keep it simple and polite.** Keep the letter to one page and one point as much as possible. (Use a conversational tone—don't try to sound too official, but don't use slang terms either. Use polite, clear language.

3. **Be direct and convincing.** Write your message directly and clearly. Support points with convincing arguments and examples, if needed.

4. **Check for grammar and accuracy.** Have someone you trust read over the letter and check for mistakes. Make sure they can

clearly understand what you are trying to say. One spelling mistake will register with the intended reader and discredit what you have to say, so make sure everything is accurate! *(or should that be "accurite"?)*

BASIC FORMAL LETTER FORMAT

January 26, 2004 (date)

Ms. Angela Thompson (name)
Admissions Officer (job title)
University of Oregon (company)
Office of Admissions (address)
240 Oregon Hall (address)
1217 University of Oregon (address)
Eugene, Oregon 97403-1217 (city, state zip code)

Campus Visit on February 8-9, 2004 (Subject or attention line)

Dear Ms. Thompson: (salutation)

Thank you so much for your letter of acceptance dated December 17, 2003. I am pleased to inform you that I will be visiting the University of Oregon on February 8 and 9, 2004. I hope to be able to meet with you at that time and discuss my attending the University of Oregon this next fall. (body paragraph)

I have been looking through the materials that you sent me and am very excited to be visiting the campus in person. I look forward to meeting you. (body paragraph)

Respectfully, (closing)
Caleb Michaels (signature)

Caleb Michaels (your name) *(Hey!That's not my name!)*
23894 S. Mount Tamor Drive (your address)
Lincoln City, Washington 98337 (your city, state zip code)

 **THINK TWICE**

In our country economy, letter writing is an hors d'oeuvre.
It is no part of the regular routine of the day.

THOMAS JEFFERSON
(I don't know what that means, either!)

Little men use big words, big men use little words.

BERTRAND RUSSELL
(So . . . does that mean Thomas Jefferson was vertically challenged?)

SOMETHING GOD HAS PROMISED YOU

I urge you, dear brothers and sisters, please listen
carefully to what I have said in this brief letter.

HEBREWS 13:22 NLT

MAKE THE RIGHT IMPRESSION OVER THE PHONE.

When you are making official calls, it is good to remember some of the following tips:

- Introduce yourself and tell the person who answers what you want to know or who you wish to speak with.

- Be friendly—you are talking to people, not a machine.

- If you have a number of things to ask, make sure you have written down your list so that you remember everything and won't need to call back unnecessarily.

- Don't make unnecessary or rude comments if you are put on hold. Often people just turn off their mikes when they tell you that you are on hold, so they can still hear everything that you say! *(Oops!)*

- Say good-bye politely and make sure the conversation is over before you hang up. It is often a good idea to let them hang up first or to hang up after a few seconds of clear silence.

Here are some good things to remember when you are answering the phone, especially if it is at a place of business:

- Greet the person, telling them who or where they have telephoned. At home you might say something such as, "Hello, this is the Jensen residence. Susan speaking," or if it is at a business, "Hello. This is Mike's Burrito Stand. Mark speaking; how may I help you?" *(I'd like a taco with the works!)* If you are answering someone else's phone in an office, you might say something like, "You have reached Milo Dickerson's office. This is Amy speaking."

- If they are calling for someone else, be sure you know who is calling and what they are calling about before you transfer the call. Then don't yell out this information, but put the phone down and go tell the person or put the caller on hold.

HELPFUL WEB SITES

Web sites with tips and samples for letter writing
www.writinghelp-central.com/letter-writing.html
www.business-letter-writing.com
www.wmich.edu/library/ref/vrd/letters.html

For more information on proper telephone etiquette
careerservices.missouri.edu/resources/Telephone_Etiquette.pdf
http://www.units.ohio-state.edu/users/etiquette.html

HELPFUL BOOKS

The New American Handbook of Letter Writing by Mary A. DeVries (Signet, 2000)

How to Write First-Class Letters: The Handbook for Practical Letter Writing by L. Sue Baugh (NTC Business Books, 1994)

Telephone Skills from A to Z: The Telephone "Doctor" Phone Book (Fifty-Minute Series Book) by Nancy J. Friedman (Crisp Publications, 2000)

PUT YOUR MIND AT REST

Courtesy is rarely misunderstood.

KICK IT IN GEAR

Make a list of official letters or phone calls that you should make in the next month.

1. _____

2. _____

3. _____

THE MAIN THING

BEING POLITE AND DIRECT AND SHOWING RESPECT FOR THE OTHER PERSON'S TIME WILL GO A LONG WAY IN LEAVING A LASTING, POSITIVE IMPRESSION.

DATING—LAND THAT DATE!

THE_BASÏCS—DAÏÏÑG 101

Okay, before anything else, let's get one thing straight from the start: *The main purpose of dating in high school is to learn how to make friends with members of the opposite sex. (All right!)*

Nothing more, nothing less. You are not looking for Mr. or Ms. Right to spend the rest of your life with, you are not looking for someone to cling to and make yourself feel wanted, and you definitely shouldn't be looking for someone to get into a dark place to see how far you can go. Teen dating is about learning how to relate to the opposite sex. If you make it anything else, you are not only missing out on how to get the best out of the experience, but you may also be heading towards a disappointing crash.

Remember how when you were younger you always thought that the opposite sex was just plain "yucky"? Well, as you hit puberty, all of that changed and suddenly those you couldn't stand before start to make you feel weak at the knees when you are around them. Before, you pulled their hair, hit them, or called them names; now you feel like you want to do almost anything to get them to like you. Yes, things have definitely changed. *(And how!)* How you go about making that transition will make all the difference in how you deal with those relationships for the rest of your life, so it is good to get first things first. Then you build a good foundation for when you go to college, when you start courting, when you get married, and how you can stay married for the rest of your life.

Not that it will all be easy, but a lot of it will also definitely be fun if you handle it right! If you remember the first rule before you go out, then you can avoid a lot of the pain and the dangers that boy-girl relationships can have. *Dating is making friends first!*

THINK TWICE

Never do a wrong thing to make a friend or to keep one.
ROBERT E. LEE

Every relationship for a Christian is an opportunity to love another person like God has loved us. To lay down our desires and do what's in his or her best interest. To care for him or her even when there's nothing in it for us. To want that person's purity and holiness because it pleases God and protects him or her.
JOSHUA HARRIS

SOMETHING GOD HAS PROMISED YOU
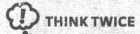

Become wise by walking with the wise;
hang out with fools and watch your life fall to pieces.
PROVERBS 13:20 THE MESSAGE

GET YOURSELF IN THE KNOW

Make a list of people that you can talk to who will help you stay focused on what dating is really all about and advise you on how to avoid the problems that might go along with it.

1. _____
2. _____
3. _____
4. _____

(LOOK HERE TOO!)

I Kissed Dating Goodbye (Updated Version): A New Attitude towards Romance and Relationships by Joshua Harris (Multnomah Publishers, 2003)

Boundaries in Dating: Making Dating Work by Dr. Henry Cloud and Dr. John Townsend (Zondervan, 2000)

The 24-Hour Counselor (online advice shorts on 24 topics teens can face) www.lifeway.com/24hour/

PUT YOUR MIND AT REST

Dating doesn't have to be a high-pressure experience, and it won't be if you don't put unrealistic expectations on it. It is really only about going out together, making friends, and having fun.

GETTING GOD INVOLVED

Talk to God about dating and ask for His wisdom and help.

Sit for a while and listen. Write down anything that He brings to your mind.

1. _____

2. _____

3. _____

Now take a minute to pray about these. If you are unsure how to pray, you can use the prayer below or make up one of your own.

Father, I want to commit my dating life to You. I will live it with the utmost respect for the people I go out with. I pledge my whole life as well as my dating life to purity, encouraging others to be closer to You, and staying far away from temptation. Thank You for Your help and strength in accomplishing these. I know that You will not let me be tempted beyond what I can resist, according to 1 Corinthians 10:13. Thank You for helping me stay in Your will. Amen

THE MAIN THING

YOU DATE TO MAKE A FRIEND OF SOMEONE OF THE OPPOSITE SEX.

THE DATE—DATING 102

Now that we have established the real purpose of teenage dating in the previous section, perhaps now we should look at what a date really is and what it isn't. There are definitely some other basics as far as what should and should *not* happen on a date to make sure it is fun for both people. If improper or unrealistic expectations are brought into the date, then it often ends, at best, no fun for anyone.

To begin with, both people should know a few things before the date begins:

1. When and where you will meet.
2. What you will be doing.
3. How much money you should take along.
4. What time the date will end and if you will need a ride home or not.

These are really basic things, but when they are left up in the air, it leaves a lot of room for problems. If the person asking you out won't provide all of this information, then it can also be a red flag that you should say, "No." Also, if the destination changes mid-date, that can also be a red flag. When things change from "We will go to the multiplex for a movie" to "Lets go to my friends house instead to watch a video," then it may be time to opt for going home. *(I have a cell phone—and I'm not afraid to use it!)*

You should also pick activities that will allow you to get to know each other such as playing miniature golf, going bowling, or attending a social event. Movies are typically a natural for dates, but how do you get to know someone by sitting silently in the dark watching a big screen for two hours?

By being up front about these few simple things from the start, a lot of wrong motives and room for misunderstandings can be eliminated and you are more likely to have a good time.

DATES THAT AREN'T A DATE

Dates can sometimes be so high-pressure that they haven't got a chance to be fun. There's the shy girl who finally lands a date with the class president and is so intimidated that she can't put two words together to make a sentence all night long. Or there's the guy who rents the tuxedo, the limo, and buys the expensive corsage for the prom only to be told his date doesn't want to see him any more halfway through the dance. When we put a lot into a date, then we can often be disappointed. Why not do the opposite though? Take the pressure off and just have fun?

Here are a couple of ways to do that:

The Group Date. Get together with a group of friends and have each of them invite someone they have been interested in dating. This takes a lot of the pressure off because you don't have to be the sole entertainer the entire time. This could be double dates or groups of six or eight. Or you might even just invite the person you want to get to know to a youth group activity or club outing. If you do this, though, don't ditch them partway through the date to be with your friends *(Right! Be nice!)*— they are still your guest, even if you never really want to go out with them again.

Informal Dates. This may sound strange, but you should really date more often. Often people don't date except as couples for big occasions, such as dances. Yet if you are not used to being with that person before the big dance, you may just be setting yourself up for a bummer of a date. So go out on low-pressure dates where you can just hang out. These can be group dates or just going out for a snack after school for a half-hour or so. By getting to know the person when it is not a "big event" date, you are more likely to feel at ease when you go to the prom or on some other formal date.

 **TH!NK TWICE**

Learning how to love, follow God, be honest and responsible, treat others as you would want to be treated, develop self-control, and building a fulfilling life will ensure better dating.

DR. HENRY CLOUD AND DR. JOHN TOWNSEND

Friendship often ends in love; but love in friendship—never.

CHARLES CALEB COLTON

SOMETHING GOD HAS PROMISED YOU

You who are young, make the most of your youth.
Relish your youthful vigor. Follow the impulses of your heart.
If something looks good to you, pursue it.
But know also that not just anything goes;
You have to answer to God for every last bit of it.

ECCLESIASTES 11:9 THE MESSAGE

THE DANGERS OF DATING DONE WRONG

1. Dating can result in your giving away what intimacies you should keep for your future spouse.

2. Dating can become your only social focus, robbing you of supportive friendships.

3. Dating done wrong can trap you in a permanent relationship for the wrong reasons, like sex.

4. Dating done wrong can affect you and your future in ways you did not plan or desire. *(Landmine City here!)*

5. Dating can set a pattern of abandoning relationships for selfish reasons that interferes or weakens your future marriage.

6. Dating for the wrong reasons with the wrong attitude can make you lonelier than ever.

WAYS FRIENDSHIPS CAN LEAD TO A HAPPY FUTURE

1. Friendships focus on common interests and can enrich you for a lifetime.

2. Healthy friendships are not exclusive and allow you to have many friends. You learn more about relationships this way.

3. It is very rare for a friendship to recover from a romance, but a romance can be enriched by beginning with a firm foundation of friendship.

4. The nature of friendship encourages patience and time to get to know one another—a nice, no-pressure zone.

5. Friendship can allow differences without rejection in a way that the dating/spouse-shopping game cannot.

6. Friendships can allow you to get to know someone before you take the next step of courtship.

REDUCING THE REJECTION FACTOR

So what if you ask them out and they say "No" and then laugh at you for having the audacity to ask in the first place?

Welcome to dating's first downside: rejection. This is why the first hints of it start with this little note that says something like: "Mary wants to know if you like her. Mark the box: ❏ yes ❏ no." We want so badly to bridge the gap and make a connection, but we also want to reduce the chance of getting hurt by reaching out, so we send a note, have a friend ask, or ask their friends who they like. In grade school those methods weren't so bad, but now that you are older, what do you do?

Here are a few things that can help reduce your chance of getting a "No" from someone you want to go out with:

1. **Be bold, be calm, be polite, be complimentary.** First of all, realize that if you don't ask, the answer is already "No," so you improve your chances of a "Yes" just by asking. Most people also respond well to self-confidence. So even if your heart is going a hundred miles an hour, steady yourself against it and start the conversation. Say something nice about the person. Then take the plunge. If the answer is still "No," then be gracious and end with something along the lines of, "Well, maybe some other time then." It could be that they are really just busy.

2. **Ask them on a few informal dates first.** You are much more likely to get a "Yes" in a low-pressure situation than on a big event. Then you can ask them out with confidence on a big event later if it is still fitting.

3. **Just do it! It is no big deal!** The longer you put it off, the more likely they are to be busy and the more nervous you will be

when you ask. Then, even if it is "No," you will also still have time to ask someone else. They won't all be "Yes," but if you do these things you will at least reduce the "No" factor. As Yoda said, "Do or do not; there is no try." *(Yoda didn't get any dates, either!)*

KICK IT IN GEAR

Here is a list of activities that encourage conversation that you could share in a group with someone you want to know better. Add some of your own at the end of the list.

1. Bowling
2. Picnics
3. A Board Game Party
4. Church youth group activities
5. Horseback riding
6. Progressive Dinners—Each course of the meal at a different house.
7. A study group for a big test
8. Your addition: *(2 + 5 + 7 = 14 Ha!)*
9. Your addition: _____
10. Your addition: _____

THE MAIN THING

DATING IS NOT ABOUT SEX BUT ABOUT LEARNING TO BUILD HEALTHY RELATIONSHIPS.

WHAT IF I'M DUMPED?

(Aargh!)

Breaking up is one reason why pursuing friendships can be a wise decision. Unless you are in one of those magical relationships where you meet the person you marry in grade school or something—and those are pretty rare—you are going to have to deal with a breakup or two in your high school years. But if you choose to date, just know breakups have happened to others and they have survived it, so you can too.

Yet knowing that doesn't really help much when you're in the midst of it. It hurts a lot to have someone break up with you. *(But only for the first couple hundred years—then the pain will begin to ease!)* Knowing that you will survive is a good first step, but what can you do in the midst of it hurting so much?

1. **Talk it out.** Being with a parent or friend can help.

2. **Remember that you are loved.** Even if you don't feel it right now, you are still loved. Jesus loves you. Your parents love you. Your friends love you. Hang on to that love right now.

3. **Count your blessings.** There are a lot of things worse in life than breaking up. Put it in perspective.

4. **Forgive the other person.** Holding a grudge will do more to hurt *you* in the long run than them. Forgive them for the hurt you are feeling.

5. **Go on with life.** Don't let your hurt keep you from going on with life. It is okay to grieve for a while, but you also need to get on with life. Besides, moving on with your regular activities can help you get your mind off of it and help you heal. *(And 6. Remember there are more frogs in the pond!)*

BREAKING UP IS HARD TO DO

As the old saying goes, "There are two sides to every coin." What if you are in a dating relationship that is moving too fast or seems to be heading more towards manipulation than friendship? How do you slow things down with minimal hurt to the other person?

Here are some things to remember when you need to break off a dating relationship:

1. **Do it personally.** It is too easy to break up by writing a note, through a friend, or over the phone. *(So I can't just disappear, either? This is hard!)* Go to their house or a neutral location and talk it out.

2. **Pray about it before you go.** Pray that you do the right thing and then pray for the other person in advance.

3. **Face the music.** Be direct and firm, but tactful. Don't put it off if you know it needs to happen.

4. **Pick a good time.** A big occasion such as a prom is a bad time to break up. If you need to, do it long before that and go with someone else. Or, if time is short, and you can, go as friends in a group so that it reduces the pressure but you still don't miss out on the big event.

5. **Be honest, but not cruel.** If you have cared for that person for some time, then you owe them an explanation for why you are breaking it off. Keep it simple. Don't run them down. Hopefully it will be a time for both of you to grow.

A lot of people get hurt because the other person is simply too self-absorbed to be courteous in such situations. Simply treating the other person the way you would want to be treated can make it easier for both of you.

 **TH!NK TWICE**

You can complain because roses have thorns,
or you can rejoice that thorns have roses.

ZIGGY

(I'm just glad my name's not Ziggy!)

The nearer you come into relation with a person,
the more necessary do tact and courtesy become.

OLIVER WENDELL JR. HOLMES

SOMETHING GOD HAS PROMISED YOU

"You're blessed when you feel you've lost what is most dear to you.
Only then can you be embraced by the One most dear to you."

MATTHEW 5:4 THE MESSAGE

HOW CAN YOU HELP WHEN A FRIEND GETS DUMPED?

↳ Let them talk it out. They need someone to be with more than someone who thinks they have all of the answers. *(I'm all ears, said Dumbo!)*

↳ Just hang out. Time is a great healer and it will take some time for their hurting to subside. Just be there for them.

↳ Don't make it worse than it already is. Stay positive and don't run the other person down. The truth is "It just didn't work out." Besides, they may get back together and then where will you be?

↳ Don't let it become a "Men/Women are jerks" session.

↳ Remind your friend that they are still a good person by telling them things you appreciate about them.

↳ You are there to help them. Don't try to turn the conversation to your own problems.

↳ Help them count their blessings, not their shortcomings.

↳ Be willing to laugh with them as well as cry with them.

HELPFUL B⊖⊖KS

Where Is God When It Hurts? A Comforting, Healing Guide for Coping with Hard Times by Philip Yancey (Zondervan, 1990)

TALK ISN'T CHEAP

"It came out of nowhere," Sam told his friend. "We were all set up to go to the prom and everything, then she just broke it all off! I thought we were doing great, and then she just calls up and dumps me!" (Wow, Sam. That's the pits! . . . Oh. Right. . . . I just got caught up in the emotion of the moment.)

Too often issues in a relationship are simply ignored until there is a breaking point. Then suddenly it all comes out, everything is a big deal, and the only answer seems to be a breakup.

As was so aptly said in the movie *Cool Hand Luke,* "What we've got here is failure to communicate."

If you are in a relationship where you never talk, can never have a difference of opinions, or can never air your dislikes or frustrations with the other person, then you are heading to an eventual crisis of some sort. Little things matter. Sure, you don't want to get nitpicky if some little thing happens only once, but if it happens repeatedly and bugs you, you should talk about it. It may be something that they thought "wasn't a big deal" or didn't even realize they were doing, and once you talk about it, it will stop. Or it may be something they want help to overcome.

Just like a crack in a dam, such things are easier to fix when they are small, so bringing it up and talking it out before it is a relationship breaker is not only more honest, but may help you save a friendship as well as be a better friend.

PUT YOUR 💤 MIND AT REST

Learning to talk things out—even fight respectfully—is a skill that will help you the rest of your life.

⬆ GETTING GOD INVOLVED

Talk to God about your breakup and ask for His wisdom and help.

Sit for a while and listen. Write down anything that He brings to your mind.

1. _____

2. _____

3. _____

Now take a minute to pray about these. If you are unsure how to pray, you can use the prayer below or make up one of your own.

Father, I know that You love me. Help me to feel that love at this time. I also know that You will see me through this. Thank You for Your healing presence and comfort right now in this place. Please also allow me to remain friends with (the other person's name). Lord, I forgive them and pray for Your blessings on their life as they go through this as well. I pray it will be a chance for both of us to grow closer to You. Amen

THE MAIN THING

YOUR RELATIONSHIP WITH JESUS DEFINES WHO YOU ARE MORE THAN YOUR RELATIONSHIP WITH OTHERS.

STEADY RELATIONSHIPS

Some people do find relationships early in life that will last a lifetime, while others may date for some time before they realize that they weren't made for each other. Either way, the pressure to "lose yourself" in the relationship or "express your feelings" in more intimate, physical contact increases the longer you stay together. How do you maintain your purity in a long-term relationship?

Here are some things to remember:

1. **Resist the temptation to be together all the time.** Don't dump your friends or forget that there are other things in life. Give the other person room to be away from you and develop their own interests, as well as taking time yourself to do the same.

2. **Continue to develop yourself, your own interests, and your future.** Being in a steady relationship can do some great things for a person's self-esteem, but there is also the temptation to define yourself in respect to your relationship more than being a person on your own as well. Continue to grow as an individual. *(Like me. I grew an inch last week!)*

3. **Have real conversations.** The greatest thing that you can learn from a longer relationship is how to truly communicate. More than anything else, be excited to get together and talk about anything and everything.

4. **Avoid being in situations that will lead to sexual tempta-
    tion.** It is easier to avoid situations where you will be tempted
    than it is to stop something that is starting to go too far. Spend
    time in groups. Limit your time alone and spend it in places
    where temptation will not be encouraged. Homes where the
    parents are gone are a bad scene.

WHY WAIT TO HAVE SEX?

Most of us have heard over and over all the physical risks of
having sex before marriage—AIDS, STDs, pregnancy, etc. We have
also heard many of the spiritual ones—the Bible tells us not to,
guilt, it is a sin, etc. But having sex before marriage can also affect
you psychologically the rest of your life as well. *(Scary!)* One of the
main developmental points of being an adolescent is learning how
to relate properly with others. Being sexually active too early in
your life can not only mess your life up in the short run but, more
significantly, in the long run as well.

Sexual activity can literally short-circuit your relationships. Too
often sex can be mistaken for intimacy. Believe it or not, this is a
big problem for married adults as well as for teenagers. When
people don't learn how to be intimate with one another—meaning
that they can bare their souls and hearts to one another without
fear—then they never really learn to be honest with themselves.
Healthy, close relationships allow us a mirror in which to see ourselves. When improper sexual connection clouds this mirror, it has
taken over the relationship between the two people as well as their
understanding of who they are as individuals. As a result, this
ability to relate to others never matures and all of our relationships
are affected.

Some people resort to sex in order to avoid dealing with loneliness, low self-esteem, insecurity, fear, and other problems that will only get bigger and worse as life goes on if not dealt with earlier in our lives. This is why God has told us to wait until we are married. It is to make sure that we are "grown up" enough to enjoy it as He has designed it so that it can be a pleasure rather than a crutch.

Thus, if you really love the other person, you will give them the time to develop and grow up rather than short-circuit them to meet your own desires. This is also why they say, "True love waits."

 **THINK TWICE**

I am convinced that the human heart hungers for constancy. In forfeiting the sanctity of sex by casual, nondiscriminatory "making out" and "sleeping around," we forfeit something that we cannot well do without. There is dullness, monotony, and sheer boredom in all of life when virginity and purity are no longer protected and prized.

ELISABETH ELLIOT

Passion is the quickest to develop, and the quickest to fade. Intimacy develops more slowly, and commitment more gradually still.

ROBERT STERNBERG

SOMETHING GOD HAS PROMISED YOU

Love is patient.

1 CORINTHIANS 13:4

WHAT IF YOU DIDN'T WAIT?

You may already have had intimate relations with your steady and you are wondering what to do. It is often harder to go backwards to a friendship once you have stepped over the boundaries into sex. If your steady isn't willing to move back to friendship, you may have to break things off.

No matter what, you can receive forgiveness from God because of what Jesus did for you on the Cross. His death covers all sins, including the sin of sex outside of marriage. But when you come to Jesus, it means you are changing directions. That means you need to stop having sex and begin living in a new way. This may seem very hard. The Bible actually says it is impossible in your own human strength. However, before you get discouraged, you need to know that God will make it possible with His strength if you ask Him. The Christian life is meant to be lived out of God's strength and not your own.

Remember this: God loves you, and whom He declares clean is whiter than snow. When you are forgiven, God declares you clean. Don't let feelings of shame fool you into thinking that it is too late for you to live right and to marry happily.

MORE REASONS FOR WHY YOU SHOULD WAIT

Boy Meets Girl: Say Hello to Courtship by Joshua Harris (Multnomah Publishers Inc., 2000)

Passion and Purity: Learning to Bring Your Love Life Under Christ's Control by Elisabeth Elliot (Fleming H. Revell, 2002)

Online advice for teens from "True Love Waits" www.lifeway.com/tlw/tns_adv_home.asp

The "Worth Waiting For" Website
www.christianity.com/worthwaitingfor

LEARNING HOW TO FIGHT

No one really likes a fight. Kids cringe when their parents get into an argument. When a husband and wife—or girlfriend and boyfriend—get snippy with one another in public, most people look away or find somewhere else to be.

On the other hand, those who refuse to fight will often give in rather than stand their ground and risk conflict. After being a doormat to others for so long, hurts build up inside of them until they are ready to explode. Then they feel the only way to avoid getting walked over all the time is to walk out. Initially they walk out on disagreements, but eventually they walk out on the relationship or the marriage, not having a better explanation than "I just can't take it anymore!" Then they take the suppressed anger and poor communication skills into the next relationship.

One of the things that relationships help us to do as teens—whether they are boyfriend-girlfriend relationships or friendships of any gender—is learn how to disagree agreeably and resolve conflicts and differences of opinions without bringing the relationship to the breaking point. The closer the relationship, the tougher this is to do because so much more emotion and past experience lies beneath any disagreement—in effect, everything is personal.

Learning to work through such disagreements and arguments—listening when you are angry, weighing both sides honestly, and not letting an external opinion or decision become a personal attack—is a big part of learning to be a loving, healthy part of any relationship.

ANGER-STOPPING WORDS

A kind answer soothes angry feelings, but harsh words stir them up.

PROVERBS 15:1 CEV

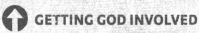 GETTING GOD INVOLVED

Talk to God about dating and ask for His wisdom and help.

Sit for a while and listen. Write down anything that He brings to your mind.

1._____

2._____

3._____

Now take a minute to pray about these. If you are unsure how to pray, you can use the prayer below or make up one of your own.

Father, I make a pledge to You, myself, my family, and my future spouse to remain sexually and emotionally pure until marriage. I thank You God, that You will give me the grace and strength to do this. Guide me and help me to develop healthy relationships with all of my friends— whether they be male or female— and to learn to walk in Your love towards them in all things, doing what is best for them, regardless of my own wants and desires. Help me to be the friend to them that I hope they will be to me. Amen

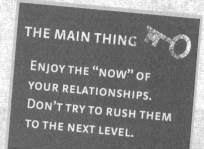

THE MAIN THING

ENJOY THE "NOW" OF YOUR RELATIONSHIPS. DON'T TRY TO RUSH THEM TO THE NEXT LEVEL.

EXERCISE—
GOING BUFF WITH MUSCLES

STRENGTH AND AEROBIC TRAINING TO MAKE YOU ALL THAT *(Aargh! Ahunh!)*

They are everywhere you go—the mall, the beach, even *(gulp!)* the library. It's intimidating. Sometimes it's downright depressing. Guys wish, *Why can't I get my abs to pop like that dude's? And look at those arms—they're bigger than my legs!* Girls wonder, *Could I ever starve myself enough to get as thin as that chick? And it should be against the law to have legs like that!*

Relax. *(Stop flexing. You'll get a cramp.)* First you need to get real about who you are and what is possible. You can't make yourself petite if you were born to be 5' 10". And you can't make yourself a major bulk if you come from a long line of string beans. *(Hey! That's getting personal!)* But knowing that does not mean you cannot improve your body.

The first thing you want to realize is that exercise can make you feel better, think better, and look better. Strength training will give you more muscle definition—and a little more bulk if you are male. Aerobic exercise will do wonders for your attitude and your mind. *(Hey! What's wrong with my attitude?)* Both kinds of training help you lose weight if you eat right at the same time.

No matter what kind of exercise you choose, don't take short-cuts with drugs, herbs, or steroids thinking you will be *all that* much faster. Some supplements can make you sterile, give you cancer, or in some cases, kill you. Crash diets can lower your metabolism and make you gain more weight in the end. Starving, or binging and then vomiting, has killed many young people. Statistics show that eating sensibly and losing weight slowly with regular exercise is the way to lose weight permanently. Reality can be so boring sometimes.

GETTING DOWN TO THE NITTY GRITTY

Aerobic exercise happens when you skate, ride a bike, run, walk briskly, hike, swim, and even do the new fad, aerobic kick-boxing. So it can be fun. And one of the best ways to increase your fun and also to exercise faithfully is to make arrangements with a friend to do any of these activities with you at least three times a week for at least a half hour.

Statistics show that if you want to keep your weight under control, you need to exercise for an hour daily; but you have to do what works for you. If you can't stand the thought of exercise, break it up and do ten minutes in the morning and ten after school. Research shows that it all adds up.

You can do strength training in a gym with a trainer, but you can also buy books that will help you work out a routine with free-weights and exercises that you can do at home. *(Sounds like really heavy books.)*

The principle in strength training is that you repeat various movements, between 10 and 20, with weights that are heavy enough to challenge your muscles and light enough that you can do all the repetitions. Each 10 to 20 repetitions is considered one set.

Often in strength training you will do three or four sets in each muscle group to increase strength and some muscle mass. This is mainly for strength, not muscle mass. *(Aww, now I'll never be governor!)*

The secret to success is to choose a routine that you can keep up regularly. It doesn't do much good to do an hour and a half a couple of times and then quit. Arrange an exercise routine that consists of a small amount of time and is simple enough that it becomes a habit you never give up. And remember the fun factor: Anything you can do to make exercise fun is going to make it stick. So have fun!

 **TH!NK TWICE**

*Take care of your body with steadfast fidelity;
the soul must see through these eyes alone, and
if they are dim, the whole world is clouded.*

JOHAN WOLFGANG VON GOETHE

*Physical fitness is not only one of the most
important keys to a healthy body, it is the basis
of dynamic and creative intellectual activity.*

JOHN F. KENNEDY

SOMETHING GOD HAS PROMISED YOU

*Physical training is of some value, but godliness has value for all
things, holding promise for both the present life and the life to come.*

1 TIMOTHY 4:8

ORGANIZING UNCLE JOHN

Sara felt like an unknown in high school, a nonentity. She wondered if she should diet until she was the size of a toothpick in order to get noticed. She signed up at a gym and went for a month. The exercise made her feel great, but her body didn't change in size.

One day her mother had her take a paper to her Uncle John who owned a radio station. "Hey! I've been meaning to talk to you, Sara. Your mom says you are a very organized person." Sara shrugged.

Uncle John ushered her into his office. She gulped at the sea of papers and folders everywhere. "Think you can bring some order here? Your Aunt Maddie says you are just the person to save me from myself." His eyes twinkled as he talked. "I won't always be around, but you can ask Bryce any questions. He goes to the school across town. He is interested in broadcasting. Bryce! Come on in here!"

Sara looked into the eyes of a very good-looking young man. "Hi," he said quietly. Then he blushed. Sara thought, *He's nervous too!*

Bryce was a great help; and it turned out that Sara was very good at organizing Uncle John's office. It wasn't long before Bryce was her good friend and soon, something more than a good friend. It didn't take weight loss for Bryce to know her value; just Sara exercising the abilities God had given her.

WANT TO GET INTO SHAPE?

8 Minutes in the Morning by Jorge Cruise, Anthony Robbins (Rodale Press, 2001)

WANT TO LOSE WEIGHT IN A HEALTHY WAY?

www.weightwatchers.com

FEAR BUSTERS

Sometimes when we want to make changes in our lives, we hesitate. Why? Because we are afraid we will fail. And these fears are reasonable ones—*we have failed in the past,* we think, *so how can we be sure of success in this next attempt?* One way to conquer your fear is to ask yourself, *What can I learn from last time that will insure my success this time?*

Sometimes the answers to this question will bring fear-conquering solutions. If not, ask yourself, *Given these unchanging circumstances, can I develop a different strategy?* For example: The person who wants to control their eating, but whose parents' food budget cannot allow special foods for this purpose, could approach this problem with portion control of the foods that are served. What if you cut your portions in half at every meal? Or what if you asked to help with menu planning to get more low-fat meals and salads on the table?

Whatever you do, don't give in to fear. Think your way around it and come up with strategies to overcome your difficulties. And don't forget that God is there to help!

FEAR STOMPING WORDS

I can do all things through Christ who strengthens me.

PHILIPPIANS 4:13 NKJV

If God sends us on stony paths,
He will provide us with strong shoes.

ALEXANDER MACLAREN
(I need steel-toed hiking boots!)

KICK IT IN GEAR

Name some things that you can do this week to start becoming healthier. And don't be afraid to name little things you can do to inch your way to a healthier lifestyle, such as putting fruit in your lunches.

1. _____

2. _____

3. _____

4. _____

5. _____

THE MAIN THING

GET COMFORTABLE WITH WHO YOU ARE AND OTHERS WILL BE TOO!

FAME—HANDLING FAME

HANDLING POPULARITY (No autographs, please!)

We may never think so, but there are some real drawbacks to having *everyone* like you. It can really warp your sense of reality. If you are not careful, you'll begin to think that you really are "all that." *(You mean . . . I'm not?)* When that begins to happen, the floor is no longer the limit for how low you can fall.

You don't have to search long in magazines or watch much TV news about celebrities to realize that there can be some real downfalls to getting everything you want. Egos soar, money flows, and too often drugs, sex, and excess become common hiding grounds for souls that just want to get away. We experience a little of that if we are popular in school; but the more people who know and admire us, the worse it gets. You would think that the answer would be to avoid it all together so that we don't fall into its clutches.

But God gave us a different example: Jesus. Jesus was the most popular person of His day—wherever He went people pressed through the crowds just to touch Him. He hung out with prostitutes and rich people—He could have had any of it that He wanted. Yet He chose another path. He used His influence and popularity to bring people to God's love, not to fulfill His every whim and desire.

How did He do this? He kept himself centered in God's call on His life. He took time away from the crowds to get into God's presence through prayer and reading the Scriptures. He had a purpose in life bigger than His own plans and desires. He focused on what others needed and how to meet that need, not on what He wanted. And thus He was sin's downfall, and not the other way around.

DO WHAT YOU LOVE

Too many people seek fame and lose everything else when they find it. Because of this, seeking fame can be like seeking wealth. Once you find it, how do you know how much is enough? Besides, are we going to make ourselves over every time our culture has a change in what is "cool" and "in?" For this reason, among others, it is better to let fame and popularity find us rather than trying to find them. *(Here I am! Come and get me!)*

How do you do that? More often than not, popularity comes to those that do what they love to do. By passionately pursuing their calling and God-given desires, people are drawn to their self-confidence, talent, focus, and vision. As a result, if and when fame finds them, it has no hold on them because they are not defining themselves by the cultural whims and fads around them but rather by what is within them. They stay faithful to the vision that is in their heart and stay their course.

But how do you know what it is you love to do? Too many miss finding what they really love because they are afraid of failing at what they try. They would rather sit around and follow the visions, callings, and loves of others rather than find their own. They won't go out for the sports team, try out for the choir or band, audition for a part in the play, submit their short story to a magazine, start the business, or join the club because they are afraid that they might not like it or they might fail. So they sit around and watch TV and admire the goals and dreams of others rather than risk discouragement or rejection.

Even if you try and fail, if you are doing what you love, you need to stay with it. Follow what God has put in your heart. There may be a time later to reevaluate whether you can make a living at it or not, but for now, give it all you've got. Dare to fail. Because without that courage to risk failure, you will never risk enough to succeed either.

THINK TWICE

Only those who dare to fail greatly can ever achieve greatly.

ROBERT FRANCIS KENNEDY

There are no shortcuts to any place worth going.

BEVERLY SILLS

SOMETHING GOD HAS PROMISED YOU

Trust in the LORD with all your heart and lean not on your own understanding; in all your ways acknowledge him, and he will make your paths straight.

PROVERBS 3:5-6

FIND YOUR DREAM BY REMEMBERING THIS

↪ Follow God and follow your heart, not other people.

↪ You are the only one who can determine what God has put into your heart.

↪ God will answer you if you ask Him what your purpose is.

↪ Don't sit around and expect your dream to come to you. You have to get out there and go for it!

↪ Do-nothings accomplish nothing.

NEED HELP FINDING YOUR MISSION IN LIFE?

Seizing Your Divine moment: Dare to Live a Life of Adventure by Erwin Raphael McManus (Thomas Nelson, 2002)

The Purpose Driven Life: What on Earth Am I Here for? by Rick Warren (Zondervan, 2002)

Life Strategies for Teens by Jay McGraw (Fireside, 2000)

Read the biographies of successful people, especially those in the area that you are interested in getting into. They often give you secrets to accomplishing similar things.

 **OVERCOMING OBSTACLES**

List the things you think will slow you down in doing what you love. *Example:*

OBSTACLE: I want to learn to play the guitar, but I don't have one.

POSSIBLE SOLUTIONS: Maybe I could get a summer job to get the money to buy or rent one to try it out. I could also put it on my Christmas/birthday list or borrow one from a friend.

OBSTACLE _____

POSSIBLE SOLUTIONS: _____

_____

OBSTACLE _____

POSSIBLE SOLUTIONS: _____

_____

PUT YOUR  MIND AT REST

*God promised that if we would seek Him
He would show us His plan for our lives.*

(SEE JEREMIAH 29:11-14.)

 GETTING GOD INVOLVED

Talk to God about the things you really like to do and ask for His wisdom and help. Sit for a while and listen. Write down anything that He brings to your mind.

_____

_____

_____

Now take a minute to pray about these. If you are unsure how to pray, you can use the prayer below or make up one of your own.

Father, I know that You have a plan for my life that is bigger than what I can accomplish on my own. Please guide me and show me the steps to take to reach that plan and start putting it into action. Bring the people into my life who will help me accomplish that plan, and protect me from those who would try to exploit that vision for their own selfish benefits. I commit my way to You knowing that You are the One to bring it about, not me. Thank You, Lord. Amen

THE MAIN THING

GOD HAS BIGGER DREAMS FOR YOU THAN YOU DO FOR YOURSELF—ALL YOU NEED TO DO IS FOLLOW THEM.

HANDLING THE PRESS, PR, AND MANAGERS

Handling the 'press is so critical that large organizations such as Nike, which sponsors athletes, now have training "universities" to help those who endorse their products to successfully navigate the treacherous waters of press conferences, interviews, and the paparazzi. Often we think that we can handle these things on our own, but when one wrong move can turn the media against you, it is good to know how to handle them. So, here are some pointers to help you handle the fame side of being famous *(I'm ready!)*:

1. **Know your vision and review it regularly.** So often people lose their way because in all of the excitement and potential of becoming well-known and rich too quickly, they forget where they wanted to go in the first place. How many say, "It was not what I expected it to be"—when the truth is that they never thought through what they really did expect it to be? Having a solid vision is like having a map through a foreign city: It can keep you headed in the right direction even if you make a few wrong turns along the way.

2. **Stick to Godly principles.** Don't give the media anything bad to report about, and they won't have anything to criticize.

3. **Get good help.** You can't do it alone. In order to keep yourself focused on your success, you need others to help who will focus their expertise in areas that you haven't got time to learn.

If they stray from your vision and principles, they are not good help! Keep skillful people around you, but also be sure they have the godly character to be faithful to your concerns.

4. **Weather the storms.** Bad things will still be said about you, even if reporters have to make them up to say them. Keep your cool and forgive, then go on with what God has given you to do. That's right. Keep your focus!

THINK TWICE

I need accountability. When you have the after-concert parties and the babes are around, I'll grab one of my managers and say, "You need to hang tight with me, because we're going into the lions' den!"

MICHAEL W. SMITH

The best way to handle criticism is to really know who you are. The reality of our business is that if you don't know who you are, there's a long line of people waiting to tell you.

MATT ODMARK

SOMETHING GOD HAS PROMISED YOU

Without good direction, people lose their way; the more wise counsel you follow, the better your chances.

PROVERBS 11:14 THE MESSAGE

CONTEMPORARY CHRISTIAN MUSIC

Perhaps the most visible Christians of today are those that have put the Gospel message to a modern-day beat. How do such artists stay centered on their visions while also weathering the temptations of fame and dealing with what the secular and Christian media have to say about them?

The group, Jars of Clay, has been known to take a pastor with them on their road trips to help them stay focused as well as having an accountability group at home to help them discern the godly way to handle fame, awards, and money.

In recent concerts, Dove Award winner Nicole Nordeman has taken up the practice of ending her concerts by singing a worship song, getting the audience to sing along, and then walking off the stage as everyone in the auditorium is praising God. In this way there is no applause or encores.

Worship leader Lincoln Brewster had this to say about handling his fame: "In the mainstream, without great accountability and without being in church, there are day-in and day-out temptations, and Satan knows right where to get you. It is too easy to get self-absorbed." He should know—he walked away from a great career as a guitarist for Steve Perry because what he was doing there didn't honor God.

Is it possible to be famous and stay faithful to God? These and other artists believe that it is—but that it also takes a lot of dedication, help, and work.

PUT YOUR 💤 MIND AT REST

If you are blessed with fame, God has a purpose for it. Use your platform to do good.

KICK IT IN GEAR ⚡

List some people you can trust who would help you stick to your dreams.

1. _____

2. _____

3. _____

4. _____

5. _____

THE MAIN THING

STICKING TO YOUR
PURPOSE AND PRINCIPLES
WILL HELP IN EVERYTHING
THAT YOU DO.

FORMAL OCCASIONS

OUT-OF-THE-BOX PROMS

So, you've been selected to work on the prom committee and don't know what to do? How do you come up with the perfect theme that will be remembered forever? How do you make that special night the most special that it can be? *(Those things are easy! I need to know who I am going to ask! Now that is hard!)*

Don't panic! You've got lots of help, both for planning the prom and planning your own prom date. But before we start, here are a few things to keep in mind:

1. **You are limited only by your own imagination—or lack of it.** Anything is possible, if you can figure out a way to do it safely and under budget! Think, pray, and imagine. Oftentimes the most elaborate proms are done with the simplest of props and decorations put together in just the right way.

2. **You don't have to do it the way it has always been done.** Come up with a list of all the possible alternatives to choose from before you make a decision.

3. **Don't neglect past experience though.** Once you have all the possible ideas that you can come up with, ask others what they have done before: advisors, teachers, parents, kids from other schools, etc. It might be that an old idea with your new twist may be just what you are looking for.

4. **Don't be afraid to ask.** You will never know until you ask. Ask if there are discounts available, ask for people who have the skills you need to volunteer or oversee what you are doing, present your problems to those who might know solutions, and see what they say.

Get all the help you can get, and you will have as much fun putting it all together as you will the night of the big event itself!

MAKING THE PROM A SPECIAL NIGHT FOR YOU AND YOUR DATE

Here are a few things you can do to make sure that your prom night is fun and memorable:

1. **Go with a group.** A lot of the awkwardness of such a formal occasion is the confusion between a time to be with your date and a time to be with your friends. However, if you mix the two it can often be a better, less-pressure-to-entertain evening. If you go with a group, also consider showing up at the dance earlier to increase your chances of getting a table together.

2. **Start the party early.** It can also break the ice a bit more if you meet at someone's house ahead of time for *hors d'oeuvres* and pictures. Invite the parents to take pictures, and share the evening a bit more. Then when they send you off they will feel a part of it and more comfortable with the entire evening.

3. **Be safe after the dance.** A lot of organizations, and even youth groups, now have after-prom parties so that teens have a safe, nondrinking, nondrug-using place to go after the prom. This has helped tremendously to reduce the number of automobile accidents that have been on the rise after proms. Unless your group of friends is going to take their dates home after the prom, these parties can be the best option for keeping the fun

going and staying away from temptation and accidents. *(Like, see if the limo can pull a trailer containing your parents?)*

4. **Keep your parents informed along the way.** Giving your parents a call or two as the evening progresses can really save them a lot of concern, especially if you plan to be out very late and in various places. Plus knowing that they are not fretting can also make it a more relaxing evening for you, so be considerate and keep them informed.

 **THINK TWICE**

Write it on your heart that every day is the best day in the year.

RALPH WALDO EMERSON

Live a balanced life - Learn some and think some, and draw and paint and sing and dance and play and work every day some.

ROBERT FULGHUM

SOMETHING GOD HAS PROMISED YOU

Don't let anyone think less of you because you are young. Be an example to all believers in what you teach, in the way you live, in your love, your faith, and your purity.

1 TIMOTHY 4:12 NLT

MAKE YOUR PROM A SPECIAL EVENING BY REMEMBERING THESE THINGS

↳ Just because you are all dressed up doesn't mean that you have to be stuffy. *(Tell that to the turkey next Thanksgiving!)*

↳ Enjoy the dance! Too many people don't spend much time at the dance because of all the other activities that they have planned. Don't short yourself in the same way.

↳ Know the plans for the whole evening and don't go anyplace that you are not comfortable with.

↳ If you are uncomfortable with expectations, talk it out. If the guy is spending lots of money on his tux, a limo, etc., he may be expecting a little more than just a good-night kiss. Be up front about it before that night and tell him that you like him, but you aren't ready for physical intimacy. This will reduce expectations and ensure that the night will be a better one.

↳ If you are a guy, don't fool yourself that you can trust your self-control all night long either. Don't go to places that will cause temptation to peak. Staying with the group and being a gentleman will win you more in the long run with your date than being overly aggressive physically.

↳ Make sure you meet your date's parents and introduce yourself politely. It will make them feel more comfortable.

HELPFUL ⬤ WEBSITES FOR PROM PLANNING

For prom theme ideas, merchandise, estimating costs, etc.
thepromsite.com
www.perfectproms.com
www.proms.net
www.party411.com/prom.html
www.promsplus.com
www.themepartiesnmore.com/generic137.html

OVERCOMING OBSTACLES

List the things you think could cause problems during the evening. *Example:*

OBSTACLE: My boyfriend is nice, but his best friend likes to get drunk and will probably want to on prom night. I don't want to be around that.

POSSIBLE SOLUTIONS: We won't double date with that friend, or we'll make sure that we aren't where alcohol will be available. We could go to the after-prom party at the church rather than someone's home.

OBSTACLE

_____

POSSIBLE SOLUTIONS:

_____

_____

OBSTACLE

_____

POSSIBLE SOLUTIONS:

_____

_____

PUT YOUR MIND AT REST

If you are open and honest about your feelings and your boundaries, you are more likely to have a good time and avoid any uncomfortable scenes.

GETTING GOD INVOLVED

Talk to God about your prom evening and ask for His wisdom and help. Sit for a while and listen. Write down anything that He brings to your mind at this time.

1. _____

2. _____

3. _____

Now take a minute to pray about these. If you are unsure how to pray, you can use the prayer below or make up one of your own.

Father, I want to dedicate this prom night to You just as I have dedicated my whole life to You. I want it to be a night that honors you and that I will remember for the rest of my life because of the fun we had. Please take away any hindrances that might emerge to keep us from having a good, pure, and blessed evening and give me the strength and courage to keep it what it should be. Thank You, Lord. Amen

THE MAIN THING

PROMS ARE ABOUT
FRIENDS GETTING
TOGETHER,
HAVING FUN,
AND MAKING MEMORIES.

HOW MUCH BREAD FOR THREADS?

(Flowers too?!)

Have your parents ever used the line, "So, if all of your friends jumped off a bridge, would you jump off too?" *(Last time I heard that I fell off my dinosaur!)* Well, the same can be said about prom spending. Just because your friends spend so much on their prom evenings, do you have to spend just as much or more? *(Hmmm...)*

When it appears that most couples today easily spend over $1,000 on their proms, it is easy to understand why they expect it to be an incredibly special evening. Yet, at the same time, setting expectations so high can also be a major setup for a real letdown. So going into the evening with more modest expectations (as well as expenditures) can be another important key to making a fun memory that you can savor for a long time.

Things that used to be flamboyant gestures—taking a limo, getting your hair and nails done, or going to the tanning salon—are now almost expected for the big evening out. But are they really necessary? Is there a way to still have as much fun and not take a big chunk out of your college fund?

Be the financially frugal future millionaire (see the section entitled "Profile of a Future Millionaire (Me?)") and step away from what the rest of the crowd expects. Don't just spend the money because that is the norm—either figure out how to do the same thing for less or figure out another way to do it. Ask for discounts and find deals. You are creative! Use your imagination! *(Yeah!*

Imagine your wallet with money in it when the prom's all over!) Half of the time, just doing something different and novel is the key to a successful date—not simply spending lots of money!

THE TYPICAL PROM-NIGHT BUDGET

On a typical prom evening the average guy, figuring they do not split some of the costs, spends this much on the standard items:

2 tickets to the dance	$120
Dinner	$65
Tuxedo rental	$110
Corsage	$28
Transportation (limo split with 2 others)	$120
Pictures	$55
After prom	$85
Total	$583

On a typical prom evening the average girl spends this much on the standard items:

Dress	$225
Shoes	$32
Gloves	$21
Purse	$32
Hose	$4
Bra	$21
Hair	$85
Manicure	$26
Wax and tan	$70
Boutonniere	$11
Total	$527

That is a total of $1,110 per couple! And this is without any souvenirs or other miscellaneous expenses. *(Yipes! Maybe you should blaze a new trail here!)*

 **THINK TWICE**

You have to develop a style that suits you and pursue it, not just develop a bag of tricks. Always be yourself.

JIMMY STEWART

Life may not be the party we hoped for, but while we're here we should dance.

UNKNOWN

SOMETHING GOD HAS PROMISED YOU

A pretentious, showy life is an empty life; a plain and simple life is a full life.

PROVERBS 13:7 THE MESSAGE

CONQUER THE COST

For girls:

- **Shop at consignment stores or order online.** You can get a dress that's just as nice, but you can save around $100. Check the fashion magazines and make sure you know what is "in." *(Don't forget E-bay!)*

- **Make your own dress.** If you know a seamstress or are one yourself, you could make a designer dress and save hundreds!

- **Get your hair and nails done at a beauty college instead of a regular salon.** This will save you around $50 to $75. Or have your mom, relative, or one of their friends do it and save the full amount. No one will notice the difference, and you can save a bundle.

For guys:

- **Get an inexpensive black suit, then rent the tie and vest to make it a tux.** Save about $50 or so (because you can always wear the suit again later).

- **Take your own wheels.** Often you can borrow a nice car from a family member or take your own. Make sure you wash and wax it as well as clean the inside until it looks the best it can. This will save you $100 or more on the limo.

- **Take a camera.** Prom memories are made in the events of the evening, not in the formal pictures. Get some disposable cameras with flashes for you and your friends to use at the prom and you will have a whole album of memories.

PROM CHECKLIST

16 Weeks Before:

❏ Start figuring out how much money you will need and where you will get it.

❏ Guys: Ask your date early!

❏ Start shopping around for what you will wear.

12 Weeks Before:

❏ Start getting your accessories ready. If you need to get in better shape (take better care of hair and nails, for example) before the big day, start now.

❏ Girls: Figure out a hairstyle, etc.

❏ Guys: Go for your tux fitting, figure out your transportation, and make reservations for where you will eat.

6 Weeks Before:

- ❏ Purchase your prom tickets.
- ❏ VERY IMPORTANT: Discuss your plans with your parents.

4 Weeks Before:

- ❏ Girls: Pick up your dress, start breaking in your shoes, and make appointments to have your hair, makeup, and nails done.
- ❏ Guys: Confirm reservations and plans. Order your date's corsage to match her dress.

2 Weeks Before:

- ❏ Girls: Call and confirm all reservations and appointments you have made for prom day.
- ❏ Collect your supplies: camera, film, clear nail polish, extra panty hose, phone card, change, cash, student ID, tickets, etc.
- ❏ Let your parents meet your prom date, if they haven't already.

Several days before:

- ❏ Guys: Confirm everything for prom day. Get a haircut. Wash and clean out your car if you are driving. Make sure your date knows when and where you will pick her up.

The Day of:

- ❏ Girls: Pick up your date's boutonniere. Go to your hair, nail, and makeup appointment(s).
- ❏ Guys: Pick up your date's corsage. Pick up your tux and make sure you have the tie, cummerbund, dress shoes, cuff links, and studs.

KICK IT IN GEAR

Here are some inexpensive activities that could make a prom unique. You can add some of your own at the end.

1. Have a makeup session for the girls that day and invite a makeup specialist to help get everyone ready.

2. Have the guys play chef and cook the dinner at someone's house. *(Hmmm . . . make sure they can cook or it could be bad.)*

3. Go to a local park before the prom and take pictures of each other among the flowers and trees.

4._____

5._____

THE MAIN THING

SPENDING TOO MUCH WILL NOT MAKE THE EVENING MORE FUN, SPECIAL, OR MEMORABLE—BUT PROPER PLANNING AND CREATIVITY WILL.

WHAT DO I DO WITH ALL THOSE FORKS!

Now that you are all dressed up at a formal meal, how do you act? Sure, you want to have fun and not be too stuffy, but at the same time you want to look like you know what you are doing. *(Suave and debonair, right?)* Not only that, but you don't want to say something that will offend your companions and turn the evening into an argument or cause long, awkward silences. Here are some things to know before your prom dinner, or any other formal dinner, that can keep you confident and looking comfortable throughout the evening:

- Here are two easy tips for handling the silverware: 1) work from the "outside in" as the meal progresses, or 2) if you are at a formal event with adults who know what to do, wait and watch what they do, then follow their example.

- Think before you speak. You can still be funny and off the wall, but make sure that people won't take offense at what you are saying before you say anything. [See the section on "Party Talk" for more help here.]

- Don't stuff yourself at the meal. You will feel better afterwards and won't look like a pig. If you need to, have a snack before you go so that you won't be ravenously hungry at the restaurant.

- Don't forget the tip. A standard tip is 15 percent, and you can go above that if you feel the service has been great. Check your receipt first though. For larger groups (eight or more) the tip is often included on the bill. This will keep you from paying it twice.

- Make sure you have plenty of cash. This makes it easier if you are splitting the bill with others so you can reimburse them right away.

 **THINK TWICE**

Manners are a sensitive awareness of the feelings of others. If you have that awareness, you have good manners, no matter what fork you use.

EMILY POST

I believe that thrift is essential to well-ordered living.

JOHN D. ROCKEFELLER

SOMETHING GOD HAS PROMISED YOU

Those who trust in the LORD will never lack any good thing..

PSALM 34:10 NLT

GET YOURSELF IN THE KNOW

List people who you think might be willing to advise you about behaving at your upcoming event:

A friend or relative who knows about proper manners

_____

Someone you know who has been to such an event before

_____

An adult who knows all about how you should be dressed

(LOOK HERE TOO!)

Emily Post's Etiquette (16th Edition) by Peggy Post (HarperCollins, 1997)

Emily Post's Teen Etiquette by Elizabeth L. Post (HarperCollins, 1995)

How Rude!: The Teenagers' Guide to Good Manners, Proper Behavior, and Not Grossing People Out by Alex J. Packer, Ph.D. (Free Spirit Publishing, 1997)

PUT YOUR (ZZZ) MIND AT REST

Though there are a lot of rules and guidelines to proper manners, the main thing is to make yourself and others feel respected and appreciated.

HERE ARE SOME OTHER THINGS TO REMEMBER

↳ Take along extra cash so that you can help cover expenses or emergencies, if needed.

↳ Be on time to pick up your date! Being too early or too late is disrespectful. It is better to plan to be a few minutes early, then wait in the car before you go up to the door. If you are picking up various dates with the same vehicle, make sure you leave enough time to take pictures and visit a little before rushing off to the next place.

↳ Be careful when pinning on your date's corsage or boutonniere so that you don't jab them with the needle. Put the flower towards the top, then slip the needle into the cloth horizontally, back through the cloth again, over or through the flower, back into the cloth and then the tip of the needle should come back out again and rest on the cloth. If a girl has a strapless dress, it is also permitted to put the corsage on her handbag or get one that goes on her wrist.

↪ Don't show up too late to the dance. You will be less likely to get a table, and enjoying this night is the main event!

↪ Stick to curfews or any other guidelines that your parents or your date's parents might suggest. It can really ruin a lovely evening to come home to parents whose trust you have violated!

THE MAIN THING

FEEL AND LOOK AT EASE.
BE POLITE. ENJOY
YOURSELF WHILE
LETTING OTHERS ENJOY
THEMSELVES AS WELL.

GRADES—NET THOSE A'S!

LOCK DOWN STUDYING AND ROCK THAT TEST

If you are reading this the night before the test, then you are probably pretty desperate for help. We all know that cramming is not the best method for preparing for a test *(I thought it was the only method!)*, but I don't know anyone who hasn't had to do it at some time. So we can cut to the chase here: If you need to get started right away, here are some things you can do:

1. **Relax. Work quickly, but don't be in a hurry.**

2. **Go for a quick overview first.** Get out a piece of paper to use as a study guide and go over all of the materials writing down the key concepts that you think you will need to know for the test. Do this very quickly. This often helps put the task before you into perspective and see that you know more of it than you have previously thought. *(Now my head hurts!)*

3. **Prioritize.** Look at your list of key concepts. Circle those you understand the best, put a box around those you are familiar with but need to look at more, and place a star next to those you are unsure about. Start with the starred topics—then move on to the boxed and circled ones.

4. **Take good review notes.** Be brief, but try to put everything you need to know onto one or two sheets of paper so you can review them just before the test tomorrow.

5. **Do a final scan.** Review all of the materials again, paying attention to headings, titles, etc. Slow down and go into more detail on areas you still need to understand or remember better.

6. **Get some sleep!** No matter how hard you study, if you sleep through the exam, you won't do very well! *(But my dreams are the only place I even get A's!)*

THE MOST POWERFUL—YET OVERLOOKED—STUDY TIME

If I asked you when the best time to start studying for a test would be, what would you answer?

- A week ahead of time?
- Two weeks ahead of time?
- The night before?
- *(How about—"It's too late now!")*

What if I told you that if you started studying at this time, not only would it be better for you, but *you would significantly cut the time you had to study altogether?* Or that it might even save you from having to pull an all-nighter right before the test? And even though all of this is true, *almost no one ever takes advantage of it?* What would you think then? *(So tell us already!)*

The best study time available to anyone and everyone *is the time you spend in class going over the material in the first place. (That's just too weird!)*

Think about it for a minute. If you take a test once a month, chances are that you have already dedicated at least 15 hours to learning that material (figuring 20 days in class for 45-minute periods). That is a lot of time! How much study time would it save you if you really applied yourself to learning the materials *during regular class time?*

That's right. If you just applied yourself fully during the regular class time while everyone else is socializing, drawing, working on a letter to their best friend, or something else, you could actually be taking good notes, learning, and *shaving hours off of what you will have to study later!* You have to be there anyway—why not take advantage of it so that it doesn't eat up your free time? *(Cool, but weird!)*

 **THINK TWICE**

I don't think much of a man who is not wiser today than he was yesterday.

ABRAHAM LINCOLN

"A book is a garden, an orchard, a storehouse, a party, a company by the way, a counselor, a multitude of counselors."

HENRY WARD BEECHER

(Don't let Henry fool you! Books are for reading!)

SOMETHING GOD HAS PROMISED YOU

God gave these four young men an unusual aptitude for learning the literature and science of the time. . . .

In all matters requiring wisdom and balanced judgment, the king found the advice of these young men to be ten times better than that of all the magicians and enchanters in his entire kingdom.

DANIEL 1:17,20 NLT

(If God did it for them, He can do it for us too!)

MAKE THE MOST OF YOUR STUDY TIME

↳ Start well ahead of time; that way you will cover everything you need to know without rushing.

↳ Ask good questions during reviews. Learn what will and won't be on the test. Find out what kind of questions there will be: multiple choice, true/false, essays, etc.

↳ Work in silence or find good instrumental music that is not distracting to help increase your concentration. Eliminate as many distractions as possible (TV, music, etc.).

↳ Make study sheets that include all of the key information on one of two pages—if there are formulas or words and definitions that you need to memorize, put these on 3 x 5 cards.

↳ Study past quizzes, assignments, or handouts, as well as your notes, if they apply to the materials that will appear on the exam.

↳ Put things into your own words as much as possible so that you can make the material more your own.

↳ Learn things from as many different angles as you can. *(Standing on my head?)* This will make it easier to remember during the test. Put things to music, draw pictures of them, or make up a way to help you remember the concepts.

HELPFUL WEB SITES

Study guides and advise on various topics
www.iss.stthomas.edu/studyguides

Various articles about study habits and homework hints and tips www.lessontutor.com/studygeneralhome.html

OVERCOMING OBSTACLES

List the things you think will slow you down. *Example:*

OBSTACLE: I always start too late.

POSSIBLE SOLUTIONS: I will get a small pocketbook with monthly calendars in it to record my test dates. Then, as soon as I hear of an upcoming test, I will write it in that book and start an outline of what I need to study. Then I will record the nights I want to study with my regular homework assignments.

OBSTACLE

_____

POSSIBLE SOLUTIONS:

_____

_____

OBSTACLE

_____

POSSIBLE SOLUTIONS:

_____

_____

PUT YOUR MIND AT REST

Time you invest in preparing for your exams will get shorter each time you do it as you learn which study methods work best for you.

GETTING GOD INVOLVED

Talk to God about school and your study habits. Then sit for a while and listen to your heart. Write down anything that He brings to your mind to help you become a better student.

1. _____

2. _____

3. _____

Now take a few minutes to pray about what He has shown you. If you are unsure how to pray, you can use the prayer below or make up one of your own.

Father, Just as You helped the four Hebrew boys in the book of Daniel become smarter, You can help me. Help me to pay attention and learn the first time when I hear things in class, and give me the wisdom to study the right things as I get ready for the exams. Help me to remember those things that I need to remember the most. Please also help me use my time wisely. Thank You. Amen

THE MAIN THING

LEARNING HOW TO LEARN IS THE SKILL THAT YOU WILL USE THE MOST FOR THE REST OF YOUR LIFE.

(Shoe-tying is also very important to learn!)

GRADES

THE RESEARCH PAPER

(Ugh! But it's gotta happen.)

Homework is one thing—and it is often easier because you get into a regular routine of doing it every night—but when larger problems come along that aren't due for a month or more, we too often don't know how to handle them. Well, here are ten helpful tips for those bigger projects:

1. **Start working on the project the first night it is assigned.** It is too easy to put it off and start too late. If you start the first night you have a crucial hurdle cleared early.

2. **Start with planning.** Break the project into steps and then get a calendar and put down deadlines for your steps. (If you meet each small deadline, meeting your last deadline is a cinch!)

3. **Do all of the research in the first half of the time allotted to do the project.** This may well be one of the hardest parts of the process and one of the parts that most high schoolers skimp on, which hurts their final grade. Find your sources, and read the important sections carefully.

4. **Take great notes on note cards.** There are few things worse than knowing that you read something somewhere but can't find it again as you are writing your paper. *(That's why I write on my arm!)* Having these notes on note cards also allows you to shuffle and organize them into the order you want to quote the

information in your paper. This can save you time with outlining later or even replace it.

5. **Start writing before you finish your research.** Start by putting all of the elements into order and building the bibliography page as you find sources rather than at the end of the project. Put in titles and section headers and go back and develop them later.

6. **Write it in the order you feel comfortable with.** *(In conclusion, once upon a time . . .)* You don't have to write your paper from introduction to conclusion in one straight line. You can go in and write important sections first and then go on to the other sections. You may even write your introduction last instead of first. But just getting the ideas down on paper allows you the freedom to get to other ideas without losing the first ones.

7. **Use journaling and free writing to collect your ideas.** Keeping a journal along the way can help you have a log of your process that you can review later as a reference. Free writing is where you take a sheet of paper and, as quickly as possible, fill it up with anything that comes to your mind as you are thinking about your topic. It can be a great help in focusing your mind on what you really want to write about. It can also help you discover ideas that you would have otherwise missed.

8. **When the going gets tough, take a break.** If you start soon enough, you have time to take breaks in the middle of the process and let your mind rejuvenate. If the writing gets jumbled, taking a break and doing something else for a while— not other homework, but something you enjoy—can return the spark to your writing that you were starting to lose because you were tired. *(Spark? That could burn up your paper!)*

9. **Have someone else read your paper.** Often someone else will catch typos, mistakes, and problems that you would never find yourself because you are so close to the writing.

10. **Shoot to finish the paper a week early.** Then review it and make the final changes one or two nights before the deadline. If you have left the paper for a bit, then you will have fresh eyes when you do your final review. That will help you make the last set of corrections before you turn it in.

 **THINK TWICE**

Research is formalized curiosity.

ZORA NEALE HURSTON
(Imagine Curious George in a Tuxedo!)

Hear one side and you will be in the dark.
Hear both and all will be clear.

THOMAS C. HALIBURTON

SOMETHING GOD HAS PROMISED YOU

Show me someone who does a good job, and
I will show you someone who is better than
most and worthy of the company of kings.

PROVERBS 22:29 TEV

THE PITFALLS OF TODAY'S MOST POPULAR SOURCE: THE INTERNET

Here are a few simple guidelines to use to make sure that the Internet information you build your paper upon will not crumble under the critical eye of your teacher:

1. **Who sponsors the site?** Is it Bill the college freshman's Web site or the Web site of the Smithsonian Institute or the He-Man Woman-Hater's Club of Des Moines? The more reliable the sponsor, the more reliable the information.

2. **Do they have references?** Facts on the Internet should be footnoted in the same way as they should be in your paper, unless the information is from the research of the organization itself (such as heart disease statistics from the American Heart Associations site or something like that). If you can, find the books they are quoting, and pull your research from them.

3. **Verify suspicious data.** If the Web site appears to be fly-by-night, it probably is. In such a case, do a quick search to find two or three other more reliable sites that say the same thing before you use the information.

4. **Just because it is on the Internet, doesn't mean it is free.** You can pull *facts* from Internet sources, but not *text*, unless you show it as an exact quote. Either way, the information should be footnoted.

WANT MORE HELP WITH YOUR PAPER?

MLA Handbook for Writers of Research Papers (Sixth Edition) by Joseph Gibaldi and Phyllis Franklin (Modern Language Association of America, 2003)

Help from finding ideas to correctly citing references
www.researchpaperhelp.net
www.libraryspot.com/features/paperfeature.htm

TURNING THE RIGHT TOPIC INTO THE BEST THESIS

Choosing the right topic at the beginning of your writing process can be the most important thing that you do on your paper. Why? Because if you find a topic that really interests you, the research and writing will not only be easier, it might even be fun! *(You don't get out much, do you?)*

So don't pick just any topic to get that part of the assignment over with. Take your time and find something that really piques your interest and can also be turned into a thesis statement.

What is a thesis statement? If you were to sum up the entire point of your paper in one sentence, that sentence would be your thesis statement. It has to be something that you are going to prove in your paper, so it has to be a statement that someone can agree or disagree with.

So pick your subject from something that you have wondered about in class and wanted to look into deeper or something else from your experience that you can really sink your teeth into. If you find the right subject, you might even be glad that you learned something new about it!

WHY FIND A TOPIC YOU CAN SINK YOUR TEETH INTO?

A great and priceless thing is a new interest! How it takes possession of a man! How it clings to him! How it rides him!

MARK TWAIN
(Are you sure he isn't talking about chiggers?)

Now I will tell you new things I have not mentioned before, secrets you have not yet heard.

ISAIAH 48:6 NLT

KICK IT IN GEAR

You can use the following format to help you make an outline for any standard essay or essay question answer. It can also be used for longer research papers, but it would be sections rather than paragraphs and there may be more than three.

Introduction
1. Introductory sentence
2. Subject of paragraph one
3. Subject of paragraph two
4. Subject of paragraph three
5. Thesis statement

Paragraph one
Topic sentence

Paragraph two
Topic sentence

Paragraph three
Topic sentence

Conclusion
1. Thesis statement restated
2. Subject of paragraph three restated
3. Subject of paragraph two restated
4. Subject of paragraph one restated
5. Concluding sentence

(Wow! Inspiring! Couldn't put it down!)

THE MAIN THING

YOUR GOAL IS A CLEAR, PRECISE EXPLANATION OF YOUR RESEARCH IN AN EASY-TO-FOLLOW FORMAT.

THAT JOB CONCEPT

TO WORK OR CHILL *(What a question!)*

Are you looking at the option of a summer job vs. summer fun, or after-school work vs. after-school hanging out with your friends? It can be a tough decision, especially considering that you will be spending the rest of your life working, so why not have fun now? On the other hand, it would sure be nice to have the extra money. Here are a few things to consider that might help you answer this question:

1. **What are your long-term goals?** Do you want to go to college? Then what? As the ancient Chinese proverb says, "A journey of a thousand miles begins with a single step." Taking that step now can get you well on your way ahead of everyone else. *(Wait a minute! All those ancient Chinese guys died!)*

2. **What are your short-term goals?** Do you want a new car? A new stereo for your room? When your parents won't splurge for such things, perhaps your best way to your goal is to pick up a part-time job.

3. **Can you do both?** A normal part-time job is 20 to 25 hours a week, sometimes less. At some high schools upper-class members can get the afternoon off school to work if it doesn't interfere with their graduating on time. It might be possible to work and still have time to spend with your friends.

4. **Can you find a job you enjoy?** It is one thing to work, but it is another thing when that work is *work*. Are you growing at the job or just groaning? If you are doing something that is preparing you for better things ahead, then it may well be worth it—but if you are struggling to get by every day for cash you don't necessarily need, then you may well be better off refining your social skills with your friends.

WHAT IS YOUR PASSION?

What do you love to do? Believe it or not, that may well be a key that God has given you to living your life.

Psalm 37:4 tells us that if you "Delight yourself in the LORD . . . he will give you the desires of your heart." Many think that that means, if you delight yourself in God and want to go to medical school, He will help you go to medical school. That could be true, but it also could be that He gave you the *desire* to go to medical school. In other words, when you dedicate your life to God and delight in His ways, He will give you new desires in your heart. And, if you like something, it may well be your God-given mission in life. *(I like sleep! . . . Oh . . . right, not a career.)*

Of course, the Bible also tells us "When you ask, you do not receive, because you ask with wrong motives, that you may spend what you get on your pleasures" (James 4:3). Does that mean that God doesn't want us to have fun or enjoy the things that we do have? No, it really means that He can't abide selfishness. It is one thing if you want to go to medical school just for the money and prestige of being a doctor; it is another if you want to go to help others and find the cure for cancer or heart disease. You may get rich either way; one will lead to emptiness in life and the other to fulfillment.

So, in other words, what you are passionate about doing in life may well be what God is leading you to accomplishing, but if your motives are selfish, you need to reevaluate. Only following what you love with pure motives will get you what you really want in the long run.

So what is your passion? Do you want to start working on it now, or are you better off chilling for a while and building the character and morals that will keep your motives pure? This is the balance you need in order to be all that God wants you to be.

 **THINK TWICE**

*I don't like work . . . but I like what is in work—
the chance to find yourself. Your own reality—for yourself,
not for others—which no other man can ever know.*

JOSEPH CONRAD

*If you don't have a dream, how are you going
to make a dream come true?*

OSCAR HAMMERSTEIN
(And if I don't take a nap, how am I gonna dream?)

SOMETHING GOD HAS PROMISED YOU

*I know what I'm doing. I have it all planned out—
plans to take care of you, not abandon you,
plans to give you the future you hope for.*

JEREMIAH 29:11 THE MESSAGE

TEENAGE ENTREPENEURS

It is one thing to get a job working at a fast-food restaurant something similar, but it is quite another to start your own business. Look at some of the following examples of people who started their businesses out of their passions as teenagers:

- Anna and Sarah Levison brewed their first batch of nail polish at home when they were 14 and 17 because they liked playing with eye-popping colors. *(Eye popping? Sounds dangerous!)* In three years their cosmetic company, Ripe, grew into a $500,000-a-year business.

- Fred DeLuca, now President and CEO of Subway, opened his first sandwich shop at the age of 17. Today Subway has over 14,000 stores in 71 countries.

- Bill Gates developed his first computer programming language as a freshman at Harvard. He was so excited about his vision for the future of personal computers that he left college to concentrate on his fledgling company, Microsoft.

- Jasmine Jordan started *Tools for Living* magazine at the age of 12. She started with a $300 investment from her family that paid for 50 magazines that sold out the first day. In just four years it grew to a circulation of 25,000. Yet she didn't stop there— she now also runs a clothing drive to get proper business attire to struggling inner-city entrepreneurs and also operates the Working Teen Program.

WANT TO START YOUR OWN BUSINESS?

How to Be a Teenage Millionaire: Start Your Own Business, Make Your Own Money, and Run Your Own Life by Art Beroff and T. R. Adams (Entrepreneur Press, 2000)

You can also find other information and resources at www.entrepreneur.com and at www.teenstartups.com

DARE TO BE DIFFERENT

No one distinguishes themselves by following the crowd. True success is found by doing something unique—oftentimes it is exactly the opposite of what everyone else is doing. When everyone else is hungry, you sell food rather than eating it. While others are goofing around, you are working hard. If everyone else is watching a baseball game or some other sporting event, you want to be one of the ones being watched.

Of course, this is not always true, but most successful businesses become that way because they are zigging when the rest of the world is zagging. *(So zig!)* When others are spending, they are saving. When others are selling cheaply because they need the cash, they are buying. While others are looking for jobs, they are creating businesses. While others wait for opportunity to knock, they are knocking on doors to make opportunities happen. By going against the trends, they make a fortune.

Would you dare to follow your dream, even if it were different from everyone else's?

DARING WORDS

"If you are unwilling to serve the Lord, then choose today whom you will serve. . . . But as for me and my family, we will serve the Lord."

JOSHUA 24:15 NLT

You have to believe in yourself and your ideas.
You have to be willing to try things and make a lot
of mistakes. Don't look at what other people are doing
and copy that, but instead, come up with your own plan.

MICHAEL DELL
Founder of Dell Computers

KICK IT IN GEAR

Here is a list of jobs you might consider doing or businesses you might like to start. Add a few of your own at the end.

1. Pet-sitting business

2. Salesperson at a department store—choose a department that reflects your interests. *(I'm interested in sleep ... Mattresses!)*

3. Handmade card or jewelry business

4. A summer business might be starting a little day camp for your neighborhood.

5. If you are an excellent student, you could offer to tutor younger students and charge by the hour.

6. _____

7. _____

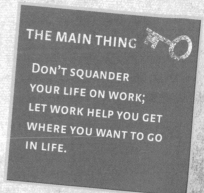

THE MAIN THING

DON'T SQUANDER YOUR LIFE ON WORK; LET WORK HELP YOU GET WHERE YOU WANT TO GO IN LIFE.

JOBS

THREADS AND DREADS: WHERE TO GO, WHAT TO BRING, AND WHAT TO SAY

HOW TO DRESS *(Yup. Those are real dreads)*

Dress code for interviews often depends on the kind of job you apply for. *(Duh!)*

If you are applying for a job at a fast-food restaurant or a grocery store, casual clothes that are neat and clean are fine. Don't forget to use the iron! Wrinkles count.

However, for office jobs and department store work, dressing up will create a good impression, and that is what the clothing issue is all about.

Employers make a pretty fast judgement based on what they see in the first few seconds when they meet you. They will talk to you to see if what you say continues to support that first image they have, but they are pretty tied to that first image. And they are thinking, *Does this person look responsible, trustworthy?* *(And like someone who won't scare the little old ladies at the checkout counter?)* And remember, the image that employers prefer is not the same as the image that impresses your friends.

 **THINK TWICE**

A graceful and pleasing figure is a perpetual letter of recommendation.

FRANCIS BACON

Regardless of how you feel inside, always try to look like a winner. Even if you are behind, a sustained look of control and confidence can give you a mental edge that results in victory.

ARTHUR ASHE

SOMETHING GOD HAS PROMISED YOU

Hard work will give you power.

PROVERBS 12:24 TEV

GET YOURSELF  IN THE KNOW

List people who you think might be willing to advise you on this topic.

1. A friend who works where you want to apply _____
2. A friend who always looks well dressed _____
3. An adult who could help you get an interview_____

(LOOK HERE TOO!)

Beyond Business Casual: What to Wear to Work if You Want to Get Ahead by Ann Marie Sabath (Career Press, 2000).

SYMS Dress for Success
www.symsdress.com/

PUT YOUR ZZZ MIND AT REST

Taking care of your first impression will do half the work in your interview. If you look good you can relax and focus on the other part, answering questions.

BEFORE YOUR INTERVIEW

↳ Showered and deodorized. *(Hey! This is a basic book.)*

↳ Light makeup for ladies, pale colors for nails. No nightlife looks. Go easy on everything.

↳ Light cologne or perfume—nothing heavy.

↳ Hair cut or styled. No wild hair dye, please.

↳ Interview outfit of conservative style and color—black, navy, or beige are safe choices.

↳ Shoes—polished, low-heeled, and conservative in style. No extra-thick soles, sandals, or spike heels.

↳ Jewelry—conservative and sparse, pierced jewelry on earlobes only. Lose the eyebrow ring and tongue stud. You can add them back in if you are hired and they say that it's okay.

THE MAIN THING

DRESS LIKE YOU MEAN IT!
(WORK, I MEAN.)

HOW TO MAKE IT OUT THERE

So, now you have decided to work, found something you like doing and can grow at. You've been interviewed and got the job. *(Not bad, but now what?)* How do you make sure that you not only keep your job, but that you also get raises and advance so that you make more money?

No matter what the job, here are a few tips that can help you stay ahead of the pack:

1. **Show up early; leave a little late.** Most employers carefully watch to make sure their workers work their full shifts, and those who arrive late or leave early are generally seen as poor workers. By simply being a little early every day and leaving a little late, you will get a lot of respect from your supervisors.

2. **Work while you are there—play later.** Discipline yourself to work when you should and relax and visit during your breaks.

3. **Work smarter.** Ingenuity is appreciated no matter what you do. If you can figure out a way to do something more easily without skimping on the quality of the product, everyone will benefit.

4. **Speak up; but then get back to work.** There are always differences of opinions in anything that you do. If there is something that you feel isn't right, talk with your supervisor about it. Be polite, and state your case the best you can, but if it is not received in the right way, drop it for now and get back to work.

If you are right, eventually things will change in your favor; if you aren't, then your managers will still appreciate your honesty.

BE A TEAM PLAYER AT WORK

Another key to making it in the workforce is your ability to work well with others. *(That doesn't mean using your co-worker as a mop!)* This can be tough, because it is not always "All for one and one for all." While some people are working to get the best for themselves, you have to resist the temptation to do the same. As on a sports team or a school newspaper or yearbook team, the team either wins or loses as a whole, not as individuals who play well on their own or not. (If you have questions here, don't forget to go back and review the section "How to Be Part of the Team" in the **Cliques and Clubs** section.)

Being a team player means much the same on the job that it does in the sports arena or club: Everyone has their part to play, and if everyone does that well, the team will succeed.

Yet it is also not just a matter of everyone doing "their job"— oftentimes one member of the team gets overloaded and needs help. If you can stay ahead of your responsibilities, then you have the ability to "back the other person up" or help them with their responsibilities.

Another factor is getting to know and gel with your team-mates. If you understand a little of what they do and the way they do it, then you also know where they will be in the heat of the action and what they will be doing. By having a good relationship with your team members, you also leave some grace for mistakes. Should you make a mistake, they will be more likely to help you rather than letting your supervisor know it was your fault and theirs.

Another thing you need to do is to take responsibility, sometimes even if it isn't exactly your fault. If your team has made a mistake, then you have the choice to either step up and take responsibility together or blame the one who was mostly at fault. If you take responsibility and find solutions, then your team will pull together more in the long run.

 ## THINK TWICE

The road to happiness lies in two simple principles: find what it is that interests you and that you can do well, and when you find it, put your whole soul into it—every bit of energy and ambition and natural ability you have.

JOHN D. ROCKEFELLER III

The secret of joy in work is contained in one word—excellence. To know how to do something well is to enjoy it.

PEARL S. BUCK

SOMETHING GOD HAS PROMISED YOU

Don't just do what you have to do to get by, but work heartily, as Christ's servants doing what God wants you to do. And work with a smile on your face, always keeping in mind that no matter who happens to be giving the orders, you're really serving God.

EPHESIANS 6:6-7 THE MESSAGE

MAKE IT IN BUSINESS BY REMEMBERING THIS

↳ People don't care how much you know until they know how much you care.

↳ Your attitude determines your altitude, or how high you will climb.

↳ Being friendly is free; being sulky and uncooperative can cost you dearly.

↳ Skills will get you a job; character will build a career.

↳ Make it fun! Everything is easier if you enjoy what you are doing.

↳ You may not be able to control all of the circumstances, but you can control your attitude and your responses.

↳ Failure need not make failures. Mistakes always precede break-throughs. *(Very bad if you are a professional ice fisherman!)*

↳ You make a living by what you get; you make a life by what you give.

↳ Jesus said, "If anyone wants to be first, he must be the very last, and the servant of all" (Mark 9:35).

HELPFUL BOOKS

Gung Ho! Turn On the People in Any Organization by Ken Blanchard (William Morrow, 1997)

The 17 Essential Qualities of a Team Player: Becoming the Type of Person Every Team Wants by John C. Maxwell (Thomas Nelson Publishers, 2002)

Fish! A Remarkable Way to Boost Morale and Improve Results by Stephen C. Lundin, Ph.D., Harry Paul, and John Christensen (Hyperion, 2000)

THE EMOTIONAL BANK ACCOUNT

Author and speaker Stephen Covey often discusses the emo-
ᵗⁱ al bank accounts we all have where we sort of "keep tabs" on
ᵗ others treat us and how we treat them. He describes it as being

like an account you have at your bank, only instead of depositing and withdrawing money, you deposit and withdraw goodwill.

Kind and generous actions build up the goodwill others have toward us. When we keep a promise, help meet a deadline, help when we are not required to, or do any other of a number of positive things, we add to the account. When we do the opposite, we make withdrawals of that same goodwill.

The balance of that account often determines how easy or how difficult our relations are with that person. If the account is overflowing with goodwill, then when we are in trouble or in a hurry, there is often a cushion there for dealing with a particular person and working together. When the account is in deficit, when we are in a pinch, we are then dealing with a person we cannot count on because they feel that they can never count on us.

In the world of business *(Hey, you can use this at school! You could use this with your parents! Everyone needs a cushion there!)*, it is important to keep the emotional bank accounts of your colleagues, your customers, and your supervisors full and overflowing. It can be a key to your success in business as well as making your work a lot more fun and fulfilling.

PUT YOUR 😴 MIND AT REST

Kindness not only begets kindness—it also begets good colleagues and customers!

⬆ GETTING GOD INVOLVED

Talk to God about your job or business and ask for His wisdom and help. Then sit for a while and listen. Write down anything that He brings to your mind at this time.

1. _____

2. _____

3. _____

Now take a minute to pray about these. If you are unsure how to pray, you can use the prayer below or make up one of your own.

Father, I want to dedicate my business life and job to You as well as the other areas of my life. Please guide me and give me wisdom for how to behave and work smoothly with others. Help me to learn to manage myself well so that I can someday know how to manage others. I also thank You that Your blessing is on my career choices as well as on my spiritual and personal life. Help me to be a light for You in my workplace. Thank You. Amen

THE MAIN THING

THE FRUITS OF THE SPIRIT—LOVE, JOY, PEACE, PATIENCE, KINDNESS, GOODNESS, FAITHFULNESS, GENTLENESS, AND SELF-CONTROL— ARE GOOD BUSINESS PRACTICES.

MONEY—CHA-CHING!
(THAT MONEY THING)

HOW TO MAKE A MILLION
(Yeah, you can start now!)

Remember the profile of a millionaire in the previous topic? One characteristic many share is that they live under their standard of living. So what do they do with the money left over from not spending?

They save it.

But the secret to their wealth is where they save it. If you invest $2,000 in mutual funds before the age of 18, by the time you are ready to retire it will have become a million dollars. *(Yes!)* How? Well, that is the secret of a lot of wealthy people. Over the long run a mutual fund often can yield 10-15 percent compared with savings accounts which yield anywhere from 2-3 percent these days. But that isn't the only secret.

The other secret is investing money in interest-bearing accounts. *(Show me the money!)* Placing $2,000 in an account at 12 percent interest for 20 years will add up to $21,785. In 53 years you reach your million, $1,120,530.60, to be exact.. If you put in money when you are 16, the money will be there when you are 69 and ready to retire and enjoy it. Or if you start with $4,000, it takes only 47 years, and you can retire early at the age of 63. Millionaires decide at 16 years of age that a million dollars, generating up to $100,000 each year in income at retirement, is worth more to them than a cheap car now. *(Yikes! What a choice!)*

But let's say age 69 is too far away. *(Duh!)* What if you want to have a million dollars in time to enjoy it? If you put away $2,000 now and then save $3,500 a year at 10 percent, in 10 years you will have $60, 968.47. *(Not a million, but not bad!)*

WHAT IS THE TRICK? (THERE IS ALWAYS A TRICK!)

One trick is living simply and saving your money. Even as kids, millionaires-in-training understand the value of a dollar and choose not to buy the many things other teens buy. *(What! No movies? No colas?)* They have long-term goals.

Experts recommend the moderate habit of putting aside 10 percent of what you earn. This is assuming you already put aside 10 percent for God's use, which is something Christians are called to do. You can still use 80 percent of your money and make progress. *(Whew!)* When you have $500 or more, look around for a mutual fund to start a Roth IRA account (many have a minimum amount requirement).

Another trick is choosing a good stable mutual fund that doesn't charge you for selling shares. You can find one of these by reading a financial magazine like *Kiplinger's* or *Money* for a few months and follow the charts to learn the long-term yields of many funds. Look for funds they call "no load" funds.

The last trick is to have patience. *(Hey! I'm a right-now kind of guy!)* Wait through stock market surges, which might yield you up to 18-23 percent in good years, and through stock market drops, which might bring your yield down *(Yeah, like to minus 19 percent!)*. The secret is that in the long run many funds yield about 10 or 12 percent or so. That initial investment begins to mount up, especially if you make that a tax-free account like a Roth IRA.

THINK TWICE

Money, says the proverb, makes money.

ADAM SMITH

Happiness is not in the mere possession of money; it lies in the joy of achievement, in the thrill of creative effort.

FRANKLIN D. ROOSEVELT

SOMETHING GOD HAS PROMISED YOU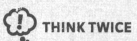

Honor the Lord by making him an offering from the best of all that your land produces. If you do, your barns will be filled with grain, and you will have too much wine to store it all.

PROVERBS 3:9-10 TEV

MAKE A MILLION BY REMEMBERING THESE THINGS

↳ Don't spend money for unnecessary items.

↳ Set aside at least 10 percent of all your income for savings and 10 percent as your offering to God.

↳ Research for a good solid mutual fund and put your money in for the long term, and don't move it every time the market dips.

↳ Increase your savings yield by investing in a tax-free IRA.

↳ Get a financial advisor, but beware of conflicts of interest when they make money just by buying and selling for you.

HELPFUL WEB SITES

This calculator can tell you how long it will take to become a millionaire: cgi.money.cnn.com/tools/million-aire/millionaire.html

CNN's site for Personal Finance information: money.cnn.com/pf/

The Motley Fool is an offbeat site for would-be investors: www.fool.com/

If you want to play with dollar amounts and interest amounts, you can go to this Web site: www.free2explore.com/compound/compounding_interest.html.

HELPFUL BOOKS

The Richest Man in Babylon by George S. Clason (Signet Books, 2002 (reissue).

The Storehouse Principle by Van Crouch and Al Jandl (CrossStaff Publishing, 2003)

The Motley Fool Investment Guide for Teens: Eight Steps to Having More Money Than Your Parents Ever Dreamed Of by David and Tom Gardner (Fireside, 2002)

OVERCOMING OBSTACLES

List the things you think will slow you down. *Example:*

OBSTACLE: No income

POSSIBLE SOLUTIONS: Maybe I could get a summer job. Maybe I could negotiate with my parents for an allowance in exchange for doing certain chores. Or maybe I could use my skills to make things to sell to my friends and neighbors. (Perhaps I could sell my stuff on E-bay!)

OBSTACLE

_____

POSSIBLE SOLUTIONS:

_____

_____

OBSTACLE

_____

POSSIBLE SOLUTIONS:

_____

_____

PUT YOUR 💤 MIND AT REST

Always put a portion of your income aside for investments, and you will find it mounts up in no time.

🔼 GETTING GOD INVOLVED

Talk to God about creating financial stability for your future and ask for His wisdom and help. Then sit for a while and listen. Write down anything that He brings to your mind at this time.

1._____

2._____

3._____

Now take a minute to pray about these. If you are unsure how to pray, you can use the prayer below or make up one of your own.

Father, I would like to be wisely responsible with my money. I want to save a portion and have that portion grow with the proper investments. I see difficulties in saving since I don't have much money coming in. Please teach me what You think I need to know. Thank You for listening to me. Now I'll sit here quietly and listen to You. Help me to know Your voice and to follow Your instructions. Amen

THE MAIN THING

USE MONEY TO MAKE MONEY . . . BY NOT USING IT—YET.

PROFILE OF A FUTURE MILLIONAIRE

(Me?!)

While the media is filled with stories of those who have made it big overnight—people who win the lottery, sign big sports contracts, get "discovered" as an actor or musician, or any number of other things—wealth expert Thomas Stanley tells us that they are not the typical millionaire in the United States. According to his book, *The Millionaire Next Door,* the average American millionaire looks something like this:

- They are about 57 years old. One out of five of them is retired. Two-thirds of them work for themselves.

- About 80 percent of them did not receive any inheritance.

- They work jobs that most others would avoid because they are not flashy. For example, they may be welding contractors, auctioneers, pest controllers, or paving contractors.

- They live well below their means, wear inexpensive clothing, and very few drive brand-new cars. They live in nice but not lavish homes, and the values range around $320,000. To look at them, you would not know that on average these millionaires are worth $3.7 million.

- They are meticulous planners, budgeters, and investors.

- Only one in five does not hold at least a college degree, and many have advanced degrees beyond college. They believe education is very important and are more willing to spend money on it rather than on luxuries for their homes.

They are anything but overnight successes. They worked long, hard, and intelligently to build their wealth over time, and when things were going well, they stocked it away rather than buying fancy things with it. Then they used that stockpile to create more wealth. They are long-range planners, not short-range spenders.

FINANCIAL INTELLIGENCE

So what does all this mean? That we have to wait to be old to get the things that we want? *(Yeah! What about what we want NOW? After all, you are only young once!)* Is the only way to be rich to miser money away until you are too old to enjoy it?

The push in our culture is to buy now and pay for it later—if you haven't already gotten at least one invitation to apply for a credit card in the mail, you are pretty unusual. Why is this? Because creditors want to cash in on that desire to have things NOW and are willing to extend you credit before you even have a job to pay them back. They know if they can loan you money when all you have is enough to pay off the minimum payment each month, then they have a good cash flow for a long time!

But people who become millionaires take the opposite track— they save now and pay for it later with cash. Then, not only do they wait until they have the cash, but once they have the cash, they wait until they find a really good deal to get what they want. Then, once they have waited, they often realize that it was not something they needed anyway, so they just leave the money in the bank. Why? *Because they don't base their happiness on stuff.* They would rather build wealth for the future stability of their families than buy something they don't really need.

No, they don't go totally without; actually they still live quite well and often own a lot of nice things that they do enjoy. They just refuse to waste their money on stuff they don't *really* want, and then if they do really want it, they refuse to pay too much for it. That is financial intelligence: *practicing self-control and patience to meet long-range needs before short-range wants.*

 THINK TWICE

Assets buy luxuries. . . . Too often we focus on borrowing money to get the things we want instead of focusing on creating money. One is easier in the short term, but harder in the long term.

ROBERT KIYOSAKI
Rich Dad, Poor Dad

Money is a terrible master, but an excellent servant.

P. T. BARNUM

SOMETHING GOD HAS PROMISED YOU

After looking at the way things are on this earth, here's what I've decided is the best way to live: Take care of yourself, have a good time, and make the most of whatever job you have for as long as God gives you life. . . . Yes, we should make the most of what God gives, both the bounty and the capacity to enjoy it, accepting what's given and delighting in the work. It's God's gift!

ECCLESIASTES 5:18-19 THE MESSAGE

WHAT DOES IT MEAN TO BE RICH?

We often look around ourselves—at the homes of our friends and neighbors—and wonder what it would be like to be rich and be able to have anything we want. *(That would be the life!)* But what we don't realize is that we are already 80 percent of the way there.

In the world we live in today, the average American household is easily in the top fifth of the world's wealthiest homes. In fact, roughly half of the world's population—about 3 billion people—lives on less than $2 a day (that means less than $730 a year). Considering that some studies show an average night at the prom to be about $1000, we need to realize that we are much better off then we may think! *(Hmmm!)*

The fact is that, compared with the rest of the world, we are already rich. Now that doesn't mean we can't work to earn more and build a better life for ourselves, but we need to be responsible at the same time. Paul told Timothy in 1 Timothy 6:17-19:

Command those who are rich in this present world not to be arrogant nor to put their hope in wealth, which is so uncertain, but to put their hope in God, who richly provides us with everything for our enjoyment. Command them to do good, to be rich in good deeds, and to be generous and willing to share. In this way they will lay up treasure for themselves as a firm foundation for the coming age, so that they may take hold of the life that is truly life.

Does God not want us to have money? No, this scripture says that He *"richly provides us with everything for our enjoyment."* But God doesn't want money to have us. The *"life that is truly life"* can happen only if we are rich in good deeds, generous, and willing to lay up treasure for our future in Heaven.

RICH WORDS

A devout life does bring wealth, but it's the rich simplicity of being yourself before God.

1 TIMOTHY 6:6 THE MESSAGE

*Money has little value to its possessor
unless it also has value to others.*

LELAND STANFORD

PUT THINGS IN PERSPECTIVE

After you graduate from high school and college, chances are that you will be working for at least the next thirty-five to forty years. *(Hey! That is twice as many years as I have been alive now!)* Are you really willing to spend that much of your life getting money just to pay your day-to-day bills?

In this section on money we have told you everything you need to know to start being a millionaire today. So, what are you going to do with all of that money? As a millionaire, you will have influence and resources to do a lot of things others can't. What are you going to do with all of that?

Certainly money can get you a certain degree of happiness, but it can't determine your happiness or what you get out of life. If getting money becomes your sole goal, then you will get it, but you will lose everything else. If you pursue money as an end in itself, it will become a master to you and block out everything else.

So now that you know enough to be rich, also know enough not to trust in it or make it your source of satisfaction in life. Learn to be rich in other things now when you don't have money, and then when you do, you will be far richer than you could ever have hoped.

KICK IT IN GEAR

List at least five things you can do to start living a richer life now.

1. _____

2. _____

3. _____

4. _____

5. _____

(Umm . . . Pick up pennies off the sidewalk? No, quarters!)

HELPFUL B~~OO~~KS

The Millionaire Next Door: The Surprising Secrets of America's Wealthy by Thomas Stanley and William Danko (Longstreet Press, 1996)

Rich Dad, Poor Dad by Robert T. Kiyosaki (TechPress, Inc., 1998).

The Millionaire Mind by Thomas Stanley (Andrews McMeel Publishing, 2000)

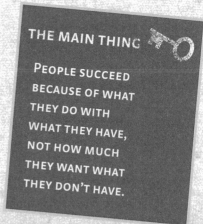

THE MAIN THING

PEOPLE SUCCEED
BECAUSE OF WHAT
THEY DO WITH
WHAT THEY HAVE,
NOT HOW MUCH
THEY WANT WHAT
THEY DON'T HAVE.

NUTRITION—EAT GOOD/FEEL GOOD

ROCK WITH THE RIGHT FOODS

If I told you that you could change just one thing and it would give you more strength, more energy, keep you from getting sick, help with your allergies, help control your weight, handle stress better, and might even clear up some of your pimples, would you do it? *(How'd you know about my pimples?)*

Well, there is one thing that can affect all of this—*eating right!*

Researchers tell us that all of these things are linked to what we put into our mouths. The convenient American fatty, processed, and junk-food diet is causing problems in teens today that have never been seen in any other generation of young people. A big part of the reason that we are sick and tired is that we are not getting the nutrition we need from the foods that we eat. *(So what am I supposed to eat? Health food? Yuck!)*

Eating healthier doesn't necessarily mean eating sprouts at every meal, but it does mean throwing out most of the candy bars, snack cakes, and soda pop and picking up fruits, nuts, whole grain muffins, and juices. It means throwing out the French fries and having a baked potato. It means cutting out so many hamburgers and eating your vegetables. Replace the bad things with good things that you like—it will mean feeling stronger, being fitter, being able to concentrate more easily, and finally losing that baby fat your friends make fun of.

Yeah, I know, changing your habits and eating your vegetables isn't so easy at first, but if the payoff is big enough, would you at least try it? Take a 30-day trial, find foods you like on the new food pyramid (see the next section), and see how you feel. *(This talk about food is making me hungry!)* Chances are, you will see the difference as well as *feel* it!

THE NEW FOOD PYRAMID
(What?! No more four basic food groups?)

Remember the four basic food groups you learned about in grade school—1) breads and cereals, 2) fruits and vegetables, 3) meats and proteins, and 4) dairy products—and you eat two or more servings of each every day? Well, doctors are finding that is not quite as good as we used to believe.

What these new researchers did was look all around the world, find areas where people were the healthiest, and researched what they ate. What they found is that people who live around the Mediterranean Sea have one of the healthiest diets in the world.

So based on this information, these doctors built a new food pyramid: the bottom level is whole grains and plant oils (olive oil is the best—no, you don't take it straight; it is used in cooking) which are eaten at most meals; then next level is fruits and vegetables, eaten five to nine times a day; nuts and beans are next—one to three times a day; then fish, eggs, and poultry—eaten once or twice every couple of days; then dairy products once or twice a day; and at the top are red meat, butter, white rice and bread, potatoes, pasta, and sweets eaten two or three times *a month*. And doctors are even recommending that most of us take multivitamins and/or nutritional supplements in addition to that.

The key is not in cutting out the bad things you eat, but in replacing them with good things that you like. Let's be honest, if you don't like it, no matter how good it is for you, you won't eat it. *(You got that right!)* But if you find healthy things that you like, it is not hard to eat those instead and find that you soon don't have the cravings for the not-so-good stuff anymore. Nor do you have to completely drop all of the things that you like. Ice cream every night may not be such a good idea, but every once in a while it isn't so bad—especially if you have eaten well for the rest of the day.

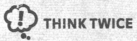

THINK TWICE

The doctors of the future will give no medicine,
but will interest his patient in the care of the human
frame, in diet, and in the cause and prevention of disease.

THOMAS EDISON

"If we could give every individual the right amount of
nourishment and exercise, not too little and not too much,
we would have found the safest way to health."

HIPPOCRATES

SOMETHING GOD HAS PROMISED YOU

Don't you know that your body is the temple of the Holy Spirit,
who lives in you and was given to you by God? You do not
belong to yourself, for God bought you with a high price.
So you must honor God with your body.

1 CORINTHIANS 6:19-20 NLT

FEEL AND LOOK BETTER BY REMEMBERING THESE THINGS

↳ Breakfast is the most important meal of the day. Even just having a piece of fruit on the way out the door will make that mid-morning candy bar look much less attractive. *(It will also muck up the doorknob!)*

↳ Each choice to eat a good food is another step on the way to good health and better looks!

↳ Get your friends and family hooked on good foods as well.

↳ Carry good snacks with you. Apples, oranges, a bag of baby carrots, or a little applesauce container keep for a long time and are a great alternative to junk food when hunger strikes.

↳ Learn to cook! A lifetime of good health can be won by learning to like cooking the right things.

HELPFUL WEB SITES

Articles from the National Institute of Nutrition about nutrition in teens
www.nin.ca/public_html/Consumer/adolescents.html

The USDA guidelines for good nutrition
www.health.gov/dietaryguidelines/

HELPFUL BOOKS

Eat, Drink, and Be Healthy: The Harvard Medical School Guide to Healthy Eating by Walter C. Willet, P. J. Skerrett, and Edward L. Giovannucci (Simon & Schuster, 2001).

The Bible Cure by Reginald B. Cherry, M.D. (Harper San Francisco, 1999).

OVERCOMING OBSTACLES

List the things you think will slow you down. *Example:*

OBSTACLE: There are only fast foods offered in our school lunchroom.

POSSIBLE SOLUTIONS: Pack your own lunch. They are typically a lot healthier and cheaper. *(Get your parents to add the money saved to your allowance!)*

OBSTACLE _____

POSSIBLE SOLUTIONS:

_____

_____

OBSTACLE _____

POSSIBLE SOLUTIONS:

_____

_____

PUT YOUR zzz MIND AT REST

Eat moderately, and major in the things you like at the bottom of the food pyramid. Know what you like that is good for you and eat it instead of the junk!

GETTING GOD INVOLVED

Talk to God about your desire to eat better and ask for His wisdom and help. Then sit for a while and listen. Write down anything that He brings to your mind at this time.

1. _____

2. _____

3. _____

Now take a minute to pray about these. If you are unsure how to pray, you can use the prayer below or make up one of your own.

Father, Please give me the wisdom and self-control to eat the things that are good for me. I know that I will have to change some habits in order to do that—please help. I also know I will face some temptations to eat the wrong things every day—please give me the strength to resist them. I know with Your help I can change the way I eat and be stronger and look better. I praise and thank You for the change it will bring in my life. Amen

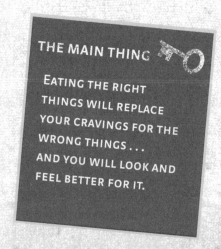

THE MAIN THING

EATING THE RIGHT THINGS WILL REPLACE YOUR CRAVINGS FOR THE WRONG THINGS . . . AND YOU WILL LOOK AND FEEL BETTER FOR IT.

FAST-FOOD FACTS

(What? We aren't going out?!)

Here are just a few quick facts about a couple of the most common processed foods that American's eat with great regularity:

- Most of these foods are so highly processed that they have no flavor left. In order to get them to taste good again, chemical flavorings are added that are hidden beneath the names "natural" or "artificial flavorings" in their ingredients lists. They are so bland, in fact, that if you wanted to, you could actually make french fries (the most widely sold food service item in the U.S.) taste like an apple by adding Ethyl-2-methyl butyrate, taste like popcorn by adding methyl-2-peridylketone, taste like marshmallow by adding ethyl-3-hydroxybutanoate, or even taste like freshly cut grass by adding hexanal. *(How about grass-flavored bubble gum?)*

- When whole wheat is refined into white flour, as in most hamburger buns, it loses 72 percent of its vitamin B_6, 67 percent of its folic acid, 60 percent of its calcium, 85 percent of its magnesium, 86 percent of its manganese, and 78 percent of its copper.

- A USDA study in 1996 found that 7.5 percent of ground beef samples taken at processing plants were contaminated with *Salmonella*, 11.7 percent with *Listeria monocytogenes*, 30 percent with *Staphylococcus aureus*, and 53.3 percent with *Clostridium perfringens*, all of which cause food poisoning and illness.

Researchers felt this was caused by stomach contents or manure coming into contact with the meat during slaughter or the subsequent processing. *(Picky, picky, picky!)*

While eating such foods is convenient and quick, we are paying with our health for being in such a hurry. While we grow fat on fast foods, our bodies are literally starving to death for the nutrition we need to stay healthy.

THINK TWICE

*Let your food be your medicine and let
your medicine be your food.*

HIPPOCRATES

*A person's palate can, in time,
become accustomed to anything.*

NAPOLEON BONAPARTE

SOMETHING GOD HAS PROMISED YOU

*Worship the Lord your God, and his blessing will be on your
food and water. I will take away sickness from among you.*

EXODUS 23:25

GET YOURSELF  IN THE KNOW

Make the decision to find out more about the foods you are used to eating now. Read the list of ingredients and the nutritional value tables for them—you can find these on the packaging, or many restaurants have these available if you ask the manager. Look into some of the following resources as well.

HELPFUL BOOKS

Fast Food Nation by Eric Schlosser (Houghton Mifflin Company, 2001)

Fit for Life by Harvey and Marilyn Diamond (Warner Books, Inc., 1985)

HELPFUL WEB SITES

Want some good healthy recipes? Check out
www.foodfit.com
www.aicr.org/information/recipe/index.lasso
www.deliciousdecisions.org
www.diabetic-recipes.com/

PUT YOUR ZZZ MIND AT REST

Eating well is not so much about "health" foods as it is about finding healthy foods that you like. Making the lifestyle change to slow down a little and eat your vegetables may not be easy at first, but you will live longer to enjoy it!

EXPERIMENTS IN HEALTHY EATING AND LIVING

Try some of the following activities to find out more about what is good for you to eat:

↳ Make up a week's menu of healthy meals that you would like to try. Pick out one of them to help prepare in the next week.

↳ The next time you have a chance, try a veggie burger just to see what it is like. *(No way! Have you tasted those things?)*

↳ Pack your own lunch for school. This can not only be an exercise in eating healthier, but also in saving money. See how much you save in a week.

↳ Have a living food day: eat only fruits and vegetables for a day (things that used to be alive not long ago and have not been processed). *(This doesn't include road-kill!)* See how you feel after doing this.

↳ Next time you go out to eat with your friends, see how many healthy choices are on the menu. Choose one of them rather than one you know is not good for you. Ask the manager for a list of its ingredients and its nutritional value chart.

↳ Go shopping with your parents the next time they go to the grocery store and ask them questions about what determines what they buy or don't buy.

THE MAIN THING

FOR REAL NUTRITION AND HEALTH, EAT REAL FOODS.

PARENTS/FAMILY—
THE PARENT TRAP

BASÏC RELATÏÖNSHIPS 101

Okay, let's get really basic:

re•la•tion•ship \ri-l__sh_n-ship_\ *noun*
1) the state of being connected
2) people or things connected or bound together
3) a state of affairs existing between those having a romantic, friendship, or other emotional attachment
4) *(A large boat containing all your relatives-kind of like Noah had!)*

In other words, things or people in a relationship *connect with* or *are attached to* one another. Sure, you may be blood relatives, and you may live in the same house, but *if there are no connections between you— no mutual understanding and respect—then you don't have a relationship.*

What is the essence of human connecting—the foundation beneath mutual understanding and respect? *Communication. (You mean talking?)*

All solid relationships start with *real* communication. This is more than just knowing where each other is at any time or talking over your day at the dinner table; it is a matter of understanding the wants, desires, aspirations, and emotions of the other person. It is about being close to one another and working together to help each other fulfill God's dream for them. This seldom happens accidentally. It is a matter of making time to really talk and connect with one another. Real conversation is not one-sided.

There are a lot of characteristics that determine the quality of a relationship: trust, openness, respect, and love are some of those at the top of the list. If you are concerned about having a better relationship with your parents—having more trust, respect, or love between you—then maybe it is time for you to sit down and *really* talk with them.

CHILDREN, HONOR YOUR PARENTS

Whether we like it or not, "honor your parents" pretty much sums up the Bible's position on how you are to behave on your side of the generation gap. Times change, but Godly principles don't. This statement is just as true today as when God carved it into Moses' tablets. Yet it is also the first commandment with a promise attached to it. As Exodus 20:12 says, "Honor your father and your mother, so that you may live long in the land the Lord your God is giving you."

Why is God so one-sided? He isn't. Notice that the promise attached to it is for you, not your parents.

You see, God designed the parent-child relationship as a way of preparing you for a long, satisfying life. As you grew up, your parents were a place of protection and security for you. However, now you are getting the desire to come out from under their protection and be your own person. *(I call it the "urge to emerge"!)* But the commandment doesn't change. Whether you agree with them or not, you are still to obey and honor them. Why? Because just as in any new endeavor, you are bound to make mistakes, and life mistakes that are made in your teen years can destroy your plans for the rest of your life. Regardless of how "dumb" you think your parents are, they have been through what you are going through now, and they know how to avoid the pitfalls. By following their guidance, you can save yourself a lot of trouble.

Yet God didn't just say "Obey your parents." He also said, "Honor your parents." This means to look up to them and respect what they say, whether you like it or not. So if you come to a point of disagreement, if you listen first and carefully try to understand what they are saying and why they are saying it, then you might just learn something. If you still disagree, your attitude of "honoring them" will allow for more discussion than arguing would have. God wants to keep your relationship whole so that you are blessed by it.

THINK TWICE

The family is our refuge and our springboard; nourished on it, we can advance to new horizons. In every conceivable manner, the family is link to our past, bridge to our future.

ALEX HALEY

Your family and your love must be cultivated like a garden. Time, effort, and imagination must be summoned constantly to keep any relationship flourishing and growing.

JIM ROHN

SOMETHING GOD HAS PROMISED YOU

"Honor your father and mother"—which is the first commandment with a promise—"that it may go well with you and that you may enjoy long life on the earth."

EPHESIANS 6:2-3

PARENTS & FAMILY

TALKING IT OUT

"You never let me do anything!" Tori screamed and then ran to her room and slammed the door. Throwing herself onto her bed, she grabbed her pillow and tried to smother her tears. It didn't seem to work though.

It seemed as if she cried for hours, though in fact it was maybe ten or fifteen minutes. Then came the inevitable knock on the door. "Tori?" It was her dad. "Tori, can I come in?"

At first she didn't answer, but she could tell he wasn't going anywhere. "Yeah, I guess," she said finally.

The door opened and her dad came in, pulled over the chair from her desk, and sat down. "I'm sorry that you are so mad," he started.

"It's just not fair!" she blurted out, then she caught herself, remembering what she had heard at youth group last week about honoring her parents before you overreact. She thought about that for an instant and then said quietly, "I just don't understand. Why won't you ever let me do anything?"

"I would be glad to explain if you would be willing to listen."

Tori thought about this for a moment. Then she sat up, wiped her eyes, and looked at her dad for the first time since he had come into the room. "Okay," she said. "I'm listening."

With that, Tori and her father had the first real conversation they had had in some time.

WANT HELP RELATING?

Closing the Gap: A Strategy for Bringing Parents and Teens Together by Jay McGraw (Fireside, 2001)

BREAKING THE SILENCE

Pick a good time that you can get together with your mom or dad one-on-one to talk. Pick a time so you have a couple of hours that you can hang out together. Here are some topics that might help to start some real conversations with your parents:

↳ Talk about a favorite book you have both read or a movie you saw together and why you liked it. Do the characters in it remind you of anyone in your family? If your family were in it, how would they have reacted?

↳ Have them tell you a story or two from their teen years that you have never heard before. Ask questions about it.

↳ What did they want to do with their lives when they were your age? *(They had lives?)* Why did their goals change or how did they bring their dream about?

↳ Talk about what you both hope to do during the rest of your life. Talk about your dreams and ask them about theirs. What are their aspirations for you?

↳ What are the biggest frustrations that each of you are facing in your lives right now? Discuss ways that you can help each other solve them. *(I'll talk to your boss about that raise, dad!)*

SILENCE BREAKING WORDS

*Listen, my child, to what your father teaches you.
Don't neglect your mother's teaching. What you learn from
them will crown you with grace and clothe you with honor.*

PROVERBS 1:8-9 NLT

The power to meaningfully changed lives depends . . .
on connecting, on bringing two people
into the experience of a shared life.

LARRY CRABB

KICK IT IN GEAR

Here are some things that you may want to ask your parents in order to get to know them better. You can add some of your own at the end.

1. How did you two meet?

2. If money were no object, what would you want to do right now?

3. How did you and your parents get along when you were my age?

4.

5.

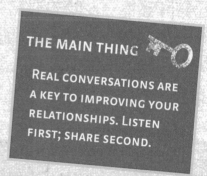

THE MAIN THING

REAL CONVERSATIONS ARE A KEY TO IMPROVING YOUR RELATIONSHIPS. LISTEN FIRST; SHARE SECOND.

NOT JUST RIVALS

They get into your stuff, borrow your clothes without asking, bug you when your friends are over, and generally mess with your life—did God give us brothers and sisters just to torment us or what? *(I think the answer is "or what," but the first one feels right.)*

While our siblings can be a nuisance in our lives, they can also be a great support and your only real lifelong friends. Yet just as with your parents (If you haven't already, look at "Basic Relationships 101."), to have a relationship rather than a rivalry, you have to have some connection to one another. If you are not willing to have real conversations with your brother or sister, then you are bound to find yourself competing more than cooperating.

One of the main sources of conflict arises from the fact that most of us look up to our older siblings and want to be like them. That can be a problem whether we are the younger one or the older one because older brothers or sisters are also trying to figure out who they are and want the space to explore it without a tagalong.

Another problem can be that older brothers and sisters tend to want to be able to "boss" the younger one(s) around in the same way that Mom and Dad "boss" them around. This only makes for more conflicts, as parents tend to stick up for the younger ones in such situations, only making things worse.

So what is the answer? Again it comes from talking things out and building the relationship. Understanding each other's needs and wants can go a long way toward eliminating some of the frustration. Compromise. If you are unwilling to help them get a little of what they want, they will also be unwilling to help you get what you want. Recognizing they are there and talking things through will get you a lot further than trying to shut them out by putting a sign on your door and locking it.

 **THINK TWICE**

For there is no friend like a sister,
In calm or stormy weather,
To cheer one on the tedious way,
To fetch one if one goes astray,
To lift one if one totters down,
To strengthen whilst one stands.

CHRISTINA ROSSETTI

"The whole idea of compassion is based on a keen awareness
of the interdependence of all these living beings, which
are all part of one another, and all involved in one another."

THOMAS MERTON

SOMETHING GOD HAS PROMISED YOU

A brother [or sister] is born to help in time of need.

PROVERBS 17:17 NLT *[insert added]*

BOUNDARIES

One of the ways that rival countries or neighbors learn to get along is by having clearly defined boundaries. The same can work in a family. If the lines between what is yours and what is mine are not clear, there is always room for conflict. Here are things that you might want to discuss with your brother or sister and agree upon so that you both can have your space:

1. How do you let the other person know when you want to be left alone?

2. What can be "shared" without asking? If you borrow something, how should it be treated and returned; and how do you let the other person know that you borrowed it? What can be borrowed but only after you ask? What is off limits?

3. What are your rules when the other person has friends over?

4. What are the rules for using shared possessions: the TV, video games, the stereo in the family room, etc.?

5. How can you let the other person know that you really need their help or need to talk with them, even if they have their "leave me alone" sign up?

6. How are you going to solve disagreements? How do you keep from fighting? *(You can do that?)*

7. What are some things that you can do to help each other? What are some things that you like to do together? Make some room in your schedules to spend time together as well as apart.

PUT YOUR 💤 MIND AT REST

By talking it out and setting boundaries that you both agree on, you can turn your rival into one of your greatest supporters.

KICK IT IN GEAR

For future reference, list some of your most important rules with your brother(s) and/or sister(s).

1. _____

2. _____

3. _____

4. _____

THE MAIN THING 🔑

BEING FAMILY MEANS THAT YOU ARE ULTIMATELY ALL IN IT TOGETHER, SO MAKE THE BEST OF IT!

HOW TO HANDLE A DIFFERENCE OF OPINION

While having a good relationship will go a long way toward reducing conflict in your home, it won't solve all of your problems. There will still be times when the answer is "NO!" and you want it to be "Yes." How do you handle it when you don't see eye-to-eye with your parents? Here are six suggestions:

1. **Take a breather.** Don't press the point right away, especially if things have become heated. By taking a break and letting things cool off, you can think more clearly to argue your point again later. *(Inhale! Exhale! Inhale . . .)*

2. **Choose your battles.** Think about whether pushing this further is really worth it or not. Is it that important? You are bound to win some and lose some, so losing this one now and obeying your parents on this one may help to get a "No" reversed later when it is something you *really* want.

3. **Consider their opinion carefully and realistically.** Believe it or not, they just might be right! *(Hey! Whose side are you on?)* But also looking at it from their point of view can help you think of better arguments to convince them to change their minds when you talk about it again. If you don't understand their position, ask.

4. **Ask again.** Sometimes just asking again politely can get you a different answer.

5. **Make them an offer they can't refuse.** "I will do *this*, if you let me do *that*." Bargain a little. If you help them out with something they need done, they are more likely to let you do something you want to do.

6. **Be "win-win" all the time.** Don't just get what you want, but help them get what they want as well. If you can do this all the time, you will get more Yeses in the long run.

WHAT NOT TO DO WHEN THE ANSWER IS "NO!"

Just as there are some things that you can do to reverse your parents' "No," there are also some things you can do that will hurt your chances of ever getting a "Yes" as well as making Noes more likely in the future. Here are half a dozen "don'ts" of negotiating with parents:

1. **Don't simply go and ask the other parent.** You may get a "Yes" in the short run from doing this, but you are setting yourself up not to be trusted, and you will get more "No's" in the future.

2. **Don't nag and badger.** Yes, you can wear your parents down in this way, but again, you will lose in the long run.

3. **Don't just do it without asking.** Some people think that it is easier to ask for forgiveness than permission. Doing this again sets you up as immature and untrustworthy.

4. **Don't sulk or try to manipulate them with tears.** Sure, it might work this time, but you are again hurting yourself in the long run as well as learning improper ways of dealing with other people.

5. **Don't gang up on them with your siblings, the other parent, or your grandparents.** This is sowing long-term strife

and will come back to hurt you later. If your parents are separated or divorced, it is often easy to play them against each other to get what you want. Doing this doesn't help your relationship with them or their relationship with each other.

6. **Don't use past Noes against them.** The fact that they said "No" and may have been wrong about it before has no relationship to your current discussion. By keeping tabs like this, you are only driving more of a wedge between you.

⧉ THINK TWICE

The basic problem in a negotiation lies not in the conflicting positions, but in the conflict between each side's needs, desires, concerns, and fears. . . . Looking to [these] interests instead of . . . positions [makes] it possible to develop a solution.

ROGER FISHER AND WILLIAM URY
From Getting to Yes: Negotiating Agreement Without Giving In

SOMETHING GOD HAS PROMISED YOU

Children, it is your Christian duty to obey your parents always, for that is what pleases God.

Parents, do not irritate your children, or they will become discouraged.

COLOSSIANS 3:20-21 TEV

WHY DO PARENTS MAKE SO MANY RULES?

Rules. "Be back by 10 o'clock." "No dating until you are 16." "When you are done you either come *straight* home or call us for permission to do something else." "You cannot go out with your friends until all of your chores are done." *(Blah, blah, blah, blah, blah!)*

Why so many rules?—It is not like your home is a prison or something! Don't they trust you?

They are trying to—that's why they give you all of those rules. *(What?!)*

Remember when you got your first bike? The experience is a little different for all of us, but typically when you first get your bike, you want to go out and give it a try. You have seen others ride so smoothly down the street—it looks easy! But then you go out and wobble about two feet—and then—"Smack!"—you hit the ground, skin your knee and hands, and run home crying—*unless* your parents put training wheels on your bike. Then you sail around like a pro right away. Once you get used to that, they raise them a little. At first that is a little wobbly—you even bounce on the wheels a time or two before you get your balance, but you don't fall. So they raise them a little more. Eventually you glide along with the training wheels hardly even touching the ground. Then they take them off and you are finally a real bike rider!

Well, rules are like training wheels. However, life can give you injuries that are a lot worse than skinned knees. Parents give you rules to see if you can follow them. Once you do, and you have shown that you can handle them, they will give you a few more freedoms to see how you handle those. If you master that, eventually they lift them all and you are finally riding on your own. You have shown that they can trust you and you have the sense to make the right decisions for yourself. Of course, if you don't follow the rules, more come because you have shown that you can't be trusted. So the ball is in your court! How are you going to handle all those rules? *(Hmmmm...)*

 **OVERCOMING OBSTACLES**

List the things you think will slow you down. *Example:*

OBSTACLE: My parents told me I couldn't buy a car until I was 18.

POSSIBLE SOLUTIONS: I could start showing them that I am responsible by helping to take care of our family car when they let me borrow one of them. I could also point out that I could help them drive my brother and sister around if I had my own car. Or I could just wait.

OBSTACLE

_____

POSSIBLE SOLUTIONS:

_____

_____

OBSTACLE

_____

POSSIBLE SOLUTIONS:

_____

_____

PUT YOUR 😴 MIND AT REST

Your parents have been through all of this before you. They might just be right! So if you were in their shoes, what would it take to make you change your mind?

⬆ GETTING GOD INVOLVED

Talk to God about your difference of opinion with your parents and ask for His wisdom and help. Then sit for a while and listen. Write down anything that He brings to your mind at this time.

1. _____

2. _____

3. _____

Now take a minute to pray about these. If you are unsure how to pray, you can use the prayer below or make up one of your own.

Father, I want my parents to trust me and let me do more things my way rather than theirs. Help me to understand their position and why they believe the way they do. Give me the arguments to convince them that I am right, or the grace to accept that I am wrong. Thank You, Lord. Amen

THE MAIN THING 🔑

TO BE TRUSTED YOU MUST SHOW YOUR-SELF TRUSTWORTHY.

WHEN THE PROBLEMS AREN'T GETTING BETTER

(I don't have trouble with problems—solutions are a different story!)

Sometimes you don't get along, and sometimes it is much more than that. Parents have problems too. When you are in a home that doesn't seem to function properly, you might very well need some help—and in some very rare cases, you might need to get out of the home for a while or longer. How can you know when it is a matter you can work through together, or when it is time to go outside your family for solutions? Here are some cases where you will definitely want to go outside of your family for help:

1. **When, no matter what, you just can't talk things out on your own.** If you are fighting more than you are talking, then you need to get some help. Seeing someone who specializes in helping families work things out may be what you need to do.

2. **If there is substance abuse.** If the problems you are having with your parents are because of drug or alcohol abuse, you should seek help outside your family.

3. **If there is constant verbal abuse.** If your parents constantly make you feel like trash, then you need to talk to someone who can help you with the situation.

4. **If there is physical or sexual abuse to someone in your immediate family.** If one of your parents or siblings is being abused in this way, they may not have the courage to speak up on their own. Your seeking help may be the only way of protecting them or yourself.

5. **If there is physical or sexual abuse to you.** If this is happening, you not only need to get someone outside of your immediate family to help, but you also need to get yourself out of the place you are being abused. The sooner you do, the better things will be in the long run.

SOURCES OF HELP

Depending on how serious the problems are within your family, there are various levels of help you can seek. Those on the following list are good places to start and can refer you to others in case you need more help than they can provide. Use your judgment though. You need to go to someone who will be confidential That means they won't gossip about your secrets and has been trained to help you. If the first person you think of isn't much older than you and gets really nervous when you speak with them about it, you may want to go to someone else on the list who you respect more and is more likely to be able to help you.

1. **Your youth leader, pastor, or church counselor.** A lot of times, if you can get help within your church, that is the best thing to do. After all, those people have been called by God to help you. If you feel most comfortable going to and talking with one of them, this is a good place to start.

2. **A teacher or your school counselor.** These people are more likely to have training to help you than most other people you see on an almost daily basis. Chances are that if they can't help you themselves, they will know someone who can and will help you get together with them.

3. **Teen-help hotlines.** These people are trained to deal with confidentiality, to help you talk things through, or to get you to organizations or counselors who can help you in case your problems are more involved than those they usually deal with.

4. **Self-help groups.** There are a lot of volunteer organizations such as Alcoholics Anonymous, Alateen, and others (See page 179.) that can help those dealing with substance abuse or those whose family members have such issues. These meetings are free and open to the public. Find them through their website or the phone book.

 **THINK TWICE**

If you are being hurt by someone through sexual, physical, or emotional abuse, or are thinking about hurting yourself, you need help. . . . I urge abused children to tell and keep telling until someone listens.

FATHER VAL J. PETER
Executive Director, Girls and Boys Town USA

Do not take advantage of a widow or an orphan. If you do and they cry out to me, I will certainly hear their cry.

EXODUS 22:22-23

PARENTS & FAMILY

SOMETHING GOD HAS PROMISED YOU

Christ chose some of us to be apostles, prophets, missionaries, pastors, and teachers, so that his people would learn to serve and his body would grow strong.

EPHESIANS 4:11-12 CEV
(In other words, God gave us Christian leaders to help us!)

"I DIDN'T THINK ANYONE WOULD UNDERSTAND"

"I didn't really think I needed any help," Alec told his new friends in the support group. "Dad was the one with the drinking problem, and when he finally agreed to go to the clinic, we thought everything would just get better and better. But it didn't.

"Sure, after a month Dad came back sober, but the anger that he tried to drown before with beer now seemed just below the surface. When he came back home it was as if a lot of things were still the same, except that he wasn't drinking anymore and didn't explode at us and throw things like he used to. Instead, he just seemed angry, and we all were scared to talk to him.

"Not only that, I didn't feel much better. I was still afraid of what he might do. With every passing day I thought it was growing closer. I just wanted it all to be better, but I still felt so awful all of the time—like I wanted to help, but couldn't. I didn't know what to do because I didn't think anyone else would understand. Then I started drinking one night because I wanted out. I got really scared. I even packed my bags to run away so I wouldn't have to face it. I just wanted things to be all right.

"But instead one of the counselors from the clinic my dad went to talked to our family, and I asked him afterwards if I could talk to him alone. He seemed to understand what I was going through and

174

told me I wasn't alone. That is when he suggested that I come here. That was three months ago.

"Things are still hard, but at least now I understand more of what my dad is going through and what I was going through. Understanding makes it easier to deal with, so now things are getting better."

WORKING UP THE COURAGE TO ASK FOR HELP

Unfortunately problems like Alec's are not too common. Though many go through similar experiences, most teens never ask for help and then are trapped in the same world as their parents. According to recent statistics, alcohol and drug abuse are the largest health concerns facing the United States today, and more than 9 million children in the U.S. live with one or both parents dependent on alcohol or drugs. At the same time more than half of all homicides and incidents of domestic violence are alcohol related.

If you have any concerns in these areas, you should ask for help. Even if it is not alcoholism or abuse, but you find yourself constantly down and there doesn't seem to be any help from your parents, then you need to ask for help from someone whom you trust outside of your family—and you also need to keep asking until someone takes you seriously.

You are not in this alone; the Bible calls the church the Body of Christ because we are spiritually connected to one another. When part of a human body hurts, other parts compensate for it and begin working to heal it. That is the way we are to function as well. God has put people in place to help solve these problems, but first someone needs to ask for help.

If you have a concern, then things are bad enough to ask for help. Do it today before your concern turns into a crisis.

FOR MORE HELP AND INSPIRATION, CHECK OUT THESE

Real Teens, Real Stories, Real Life compiled and edited by T. Suzanne Eller (RiverOak Publishing, 2002)

NEED HELP? TRY THESE HOTLINES OR WEB SITES:

For immediate intervention, call 9-1-1

Al-Anon/Alateen
For Families and Friends of Alcoholics
1-888-4AL-ANON or 1-888-425-2666
WSO@al-anon.org
www.al-anon.org
1-800-ALCOHOL for information and referrals

Childhelp USA's National Child Abuse Hotline
1-800-4-A-CHILD or 1-800-422-4453
www.childhelpusa.org

National Sexual Assault Hotline (RAINN)
1-800-656-4673 (HOPE)
www.rainn.org

National Domestic Violence/Abuse Hotline
1-800-799-SAFE or 1-800-799-7233
1-800-787-3224 TDD
(telephone number for the hearing impaired)
www.ndvh.org

National Runaway Hotline/National Runaway Foundation
1-800-621-4000
1-800-621-0394 TDD
(telephone number for the hearing impaired)

National Hope Line Network
1-800-SUICIDE or 1-800-784-2433

THE MAIN THING

IF THINGS ARE
OUT OF CONTROL,
GET HELP.

PRAYING FOR YOUR PARENTS MAKES MIRACLES HAPPEN!

(Ya gotta trust me on this!)

Too many people think, *Well, I have tried everything else—I might as well pray!* But prayer should not be our last resort. In fact, those who pray regularly often find that prayer isn't just something to do when you have a problem—it is a way to get God's guidance in life and even avoid problems before they happen. Prayer is simply spending time with God.

As we pray for others, especially for our parents, we should remember that God wants what is best for them, but not necessarily what we think is best. Prayer is not a way of getting others to do what we want and manipulating them—this is praying with wrong motives, and James 4:3 tells us that God cannot answer this type of prayer. This means that in order to get your prayers answered you have to pray according to the promises and principles in the Bible. Finding such a promise and then using it as part of your prayers is a great way to show God your faith in Him!So when we pray for our parents, we should pray that they will have wisdom and that God will open their eyes to do what is right. We should pray wanting God's presence in their lives to be a solution to whatever problem we may be facing with them or that they may be facing. Or even that they may be facing with you!

Another thing that we should expect as we pray is that God will change us. Often when we go to God in prayer we are unaware of something we are doing that may be a part of the problem. One place that prayer works is in helping us to get things straight in our own hearts. If you want your parents to change, you need to be ready to change too! *(And we're not talking about diapers here!)*

Do you really want to see miracles in your family? Then start by getting God involved in your lives through prayer.

 **THINK TWICE**

*All who call on God in true faith, earnestly
from the heart, will certainly be heard,
and will receive what they have asked and desired.*

MARTIN LUTHER

*Once I heard a beautiful prayer, which I can never forget.
It was this: "Lord, take my lips and speak through them;
take my mind and think through it; take my heart
and set it on fire." And this is the way the Master
keeps the lips of His servants—by so filling their
hearts with His love that the outflow cannot be unloving.*

FRANCES RIDLEY HAVERGAL

SOMETHING GOD HAS PROMISED YOU

*This is the confidence which we have before Him, that,
if we ask anything according to His will, He hears us.
And if we know that He hears us in whatever we ask, we know
that we have the requests which we have asked from Him.*

1 JOHN 5:14-15 NASB

PARENTS & FAMILY

WHAT IF GOD SAYS "NO."

It is going to happen sooner or later. You will think that God should help you or your parents in some way that feels really right—and it won't happen that way. What do you do?

Well, the first thing you want to be sure you *don't* do is to think you failed to have enough faith or that God wasn't there. God is there for you and your parents, but sometimes His answers go the long way around in order to respect your parents' and your free will. And some important learning happens on that long road.

Don't give up hope. God is still there and is working things according to what He in His wisdom has decided is the best way. That doesn't mean you can't tell Him you are disappointed and even angry or scared. Just don't stop talking to Him. Be honest, be vocal, and be there in His presence. *(Like, "I'm here God! And I'm upset!")* Don't be afraid to ask Him to give you insight into His decisions, though the insight may be a long time in coming. Sometimes God has to grow you up before He can give you His answers.

(LOOK HERE TOO!)

When Teens Pray: Powerful Stories of How God Works by Cheri Fuller and Ron Luce (Multnomah Publishers Inc, 2002)

Prayers That Avail Much for Teens by Germaine Copeland (Harrison House, 2003)

PUT YOUR ZZZ MIND AT REST

God wants to talk to you even more than you want to talk to Him.

GETTING GOD INVOLVED

Talk to God about your parents and your relationship with them. Then sit for a while and listen to your heart. Write down anything that He brings to your mind.

1. _____

2. _____

3. _____

Now take a few minutes to pray about what He has shown you. If you are unsure how to pray, you can use the prayer below or make up one of your own.

Father, I want to have Your will take place in my family. Please show me how to change and what to pray in order to bring more of You into our home and our problems. Change my heart so that my attitude is correct and so that You can work through me to love my family. Thank You for Your promises to us in the Bible. Show me the ones I need to ask for so You can work in our home. Amen

THE MAIN THING

PRAYER CHANGES THINGS.

(Even me!)

PARENTS & FAMILY

SELF-ESTEEM—I ROCK! (YEAH!)

YOUR LOOK

(Image Isn't Everything; But It Is Something)

The way you dress and present yourself to the outside world makes a statement. What are you saying? *(I'm colorblind? My momma dresses me funny?)*

If you are presenting yourself unkempt, unclean, and in clothes you haven't washed for a month, it won't take long for people to notice you. It is a way of saying, "I don't care for myself, so why should you care for me?"

On the other hand, if you are just wearing trendy clothes to try to fit in, then it may work, but do you really want people to like you only because you look the same as they do?

Let's face it, the way you dress and present yourself—your style—is part of your expression of who you are and who God made you to be. If your dressing is reactionary, meaning that you dress based on what others wear, not on what you like, then maybe you have some things to think through about yourself. While some kids dress the same as everyone else in order to fit in, others dress the opposite way in order to stand out—but either way they are letting the crowd dictate who they are rather than discovering that for themselves. *(I'm unique! Just like everybody else!)*

Finding your style is part of finding yourself. You should be neat and clean most of the time, but you should also take the time to figure out what you like and don't like for yourself. You don't have to be the same every day either. Go and have fun shopping for new things and new looks with your family and friends. Just remember that the image you present to the world should always be the best you can be—so keep it clean, modest, and fun, remembering that you are still the representative of God wherever you go. Be a light! *(Check those light bulbs, folks!)*

 THINK TWICE *(THRICE)*

Clothes and manners do not make the man; but when he is made, they greatly improve his appearance.

HENRY WARD BEECHER

Even I don't wake up looking like Cindy Crawford.

CINDY CRAWFORD
(Beauty is only skin deep but ugly is to the bone! -Some Ugly Guy)

SOMETHING GOD HAS PROMISED YOU

When the time was up, they looked healthier and stronger than all those who had been eating the royal food.

DANIEL 1:15 TEV

Esther, just as she was, won the admiration of everyone who saw her.

ESTHER 2:15 THE MESSAGE

A LOOK IN THE MIRROR

We've all done it—stared into the mirror compiling an extensive list of all the things that are wrong with us: too fat, too thin, big ears, big nose, puffy cheeks, crooked teeth, or any of a number of other things that we find aren't quite perfect about ourselves. If anyone asks, we would be glad to list them, but the funny thing is that no one ever asks. Have you ever wondered why? *(They don't want to make me cry!)*

Probably because most of the people we hang out with—or don't hang out with—don't stick with us because of the way we look, but because of the connection they make with the person within us. Sure, there are the popular kids who all seem to look like models and wear the right clothes, but if you asked them what they think when they look in their mirrors every morning, their list of imperfections would probably rival yours. And the only *real* friends they have are those that connect with them from the inside, not those who hang out with them because of the way they look.

Face it: we live in a culture that is image driven. We put only the brightest and most beautiful on our magazine covers, TV shows, and billboard advertisements because image gets attention. But the other side of the coin is that image does not help us to have real relationships and true friendships. Building our self-image on outward appearance is a lot like walking on thin ice: it seems fine until you break through the surface, and then it is no longer the surface that you notice but what was under it all along!

True beauty shines from within and outshines all that is on the surface. Our outward appearance then is only a reflection of our inner confidence and love for ourselves. So work on getting noticed from the inside out!

PUT YOUR  MIND AT REST

Get noticed for who you are, not for what you wear.

KICK IT IN GEAR

Here are some things you can do to look like the real you:

1. Have a friend help you figure out what colors and styles look best on you. You can help them do the same.

2. Think about your personality. Are you conservative and classic? adventurous and arty? laid back and casual? What looks reflect the kind of person you are? Look around for examples that fit you.

3. Before you buy an item, ask yourself these questions: Am I buying this because someone I admire wears one? Does this style flatter me? Does the catalog model have a similar build and coloring as I do? Is this really what I wanted today? *(Can I get somebody else to buy this for me?)*

4. How much time do you want to spend on personal appearance? If you are not into primping, go for easy-care clothing and a blow-dry hair style. Some looks consume too much time especially if you like to spend time on other things.

CHECK OUT THESE BOOKS AS WELL

No Body's Perfect: Stories by Teens about Body Image, Self-Acceptance, and the Search for Identity by Kimberly Kirberger (Scholastic, 2003)

Beauty by the Book: Seeing Yourself as God Sees You by Nancy Stafford (Multnomah Publishers, 2002)

THE MAIN THING

PRESENT TO THE WORLD THE BEST YOU THAT YOU CAN.

BEHIND CLOSED DOORS

(Will the Real me Please Step Forward?)

Who are you, *really?*

That can be a tough question for anyone to answer. Sometimes we find ourselves to be quite different people depending on who we are with, whether it be our parents, our friends, our classmates, people in our youth group, or when we are all by ourselves. It's not that we have multiple personalities, it's just that we act so differently in different situations. Which of these is really us? *(I'm the nice one!)*

The Bible tells us that as a person thinks in their heart, so they are. (See Proverbs 23:7.) Whether we act out of a need to fit in or to love others with God's love is a heart issue. We either react to the influences of the outside world or act from the resolve of our inside world. Yet too many of us never take the time to develop that internal resolve. We let ourselves be shaped more by the opinions and desires of others rather than what God has put into our hearts.

Finding the real us is a process of discovering what God has put into our hearts and letting it come out. Too often it is the other way around: What is in our hearts is hidden because we let the outside world determine who we are. *The key to finding our true selves is discovering and becoming who God designed us to be.*

That is not something that can happen overnight. It takes time away from the television, music, and others so that you can listen to your heart without being distracted. It also takes strength and determined effort to believe in yourself. It takes placing yourself in God's molding hands day by day and letting Him form you into the person who can accomplish what He has called you to accomplish. The real you is who God has made you to be—but that person can get lost in the crowd if you are not careful. *(I carry maps!)*

QUIET TIME

A quiet time is like a looking glass, a sort of magic mirror that lets me look into the deeper dimensions of life. Through the mirror I am able to see the reality of God's presence. I can look not only at God but also at myself.

STEPHEN EYRE

It is impossible to determine who we really are if we never take the time to be quiet and spend time with God through prayer and Bible reading. James 1:23-25 tells us that God's Word is also a mirror that helps us to see our true selves. It is only by taking time to peer into it regularly that we can see who we really are.

In the rapid pace of our modern world, we very seldom have time that is naturally quiet. We generally have the TV, radio, computer, a CD player, or the jumbled voices of friends and family providing the soundtrack to our lives. In fact, unless you seek it out, it is unlikely that there is any quiet time in your life at all, let alone a time to focus on God. *(What? Me, quiet? How?)*

The key to having a quiet time is making it a habit. If you can do that, then you will feel odd if you haven't done it during the day. Most planning experts tell us that it takes at least 21 days—or three weeks—to form a habit. So get out a piece of paper, mark out three weeks, and start to log your quiet times every day during that period. You may even experiment with having it at different times so that you can find what times are best for you.

Another key is to have a way of recording your quiet time. Some ways to do this are by keeping a journal, noting it in your daily planner or school assignment log, or marking it on a calendar.

If you do this regularly, you will soon find you look forward to this time with God almost as much as He looks forward to time with you!

 **THINK TWICE**

*A humble knowledge of thyself is a surer way
to God than a deep search after learning.*

THOMAS Ã KEMPIS

*Properly understood, prayer is a mature activity
indispensable to the fullest development of personality—
the ultimate integration of a person's highest faculties.
Only in prayer do we achieve that complete and harmonious
assembly of body, mind, and spirit which gives the
frail human reed its unshakable strengths.*

ALEXIS CARREL

SOMETHING GOD HAS PROMISED YOU

*I am confident of this very thing, that He who began a good
work in you will perfect it until the day of Christ Jesus..*

PHILIPPIANS 1:6 NASB

HERE ARE SOME WAYS TO DEVELOP REGULAR SELF-FINDING QUIET TIME

↳ **Journaling.** Taking time to sit and write out your thoughts and what is happening in your life on a regular basis is a great way to explore who you are as well as develop a regular discipline of quiet time. You can also log your prayers and answers in it.

↳ **Start a program to read through the entire Bible in a year and stick to it.** Such things can often be discouraging because once you get behind it seems that you can never catch up—plus some parts of the Bible are definitely more interesting than others! (Starting in the New Testament rather than the Old Testament will help with this.) Develop your own checklist that leaves weekends to catch up or has no dates so that you just pick up where you left off without feeling that you are behind.

↳ **Pray without ceasing.** Paul advises us to do this in 1 Thessalonians 5:17, and it is good advice. No, it doesn't mean spending the whole day on our knees beside our bed; but it means sending short prayers to God throughout the day. Find little "quiet times" during the day to focus on God.

↳ **Use a daily devotional.** There are a lot of devotionals published every year to help guide your quiet time. Get one that fits you and work through it. *(Mine is a size nine!)*

HELPFUL B**O**OKS

God's Little Devotional Book for Teens. (Honor Books, 2001)

The Pocket Devotional for Teens. (Honor Books, 2003)

ONLINE DEVOTIONAL SITES

www.tddm.org

www.cafereality.org/devos

 **OVERCOMING OBSTACLES**

List the things you think will slow you down.

SELF-ESTEEM

Here are some promises from the Bible that will encourage you to spend time with God:

> *If you seek Him, He will let you find Him.*
>
> 2 CHRONICLES 15:2 NASB

> *He Himself has said, "I will never leave you nor forsake you."*
>
> HEBREWS 13:5 NKJV

> *The LORD is near to all who call upon Him,*
> *To all who call upon Him in truth.*
> *He will fulfill the desire of those who fear Him;*
> *He will also hear their cry and will save them.*
>
> PSALM 145:18-19 NASB

> *He will rejoice over you with gladness, He will quiet you with His love, He will rejoice over you with singing.*
>
> ZEPHANIAH 3:17 NKJV

PUT YOUR  MIND AT REST

Don't set a bunch of different requirements on your quiet time; just be quiet and listen to God.

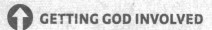 GETTING GOD INVOLVED

Talk to God about His plans for your life and ask for His wisdom and help. Then sit for a while and listen. Write down anything that He brings to your mind at this time.

1. _____

2. _____

3. _____

Now take a minute to pray about these. If you are unsure how to pray, you can use the prayer below or make up one of your own.

Father, Help me to find myself in You and Your plan for my life. Please also help me to develop a regular quiet time to be with You. Give me the strength to live by my convictions rather than what everyone else wants or expects of me, or what society tells me I should be. Thank You for helping me to be the "me" You want me to be. Amen

THE MAIN THING

YOU CAN'T FIND WHO YOU REALLY ARE WITHOUT FINDING OUT WHO GOD INTENDED YOU TO BE.

THOSE DOWN DAYS

(Hey! I Have Those Too!)

Everyone feels down sometimes. *(Especially those who pet geese!)*Discovering new emotions and how to handle them is a big part of growing from an adolescent into an adult. We never stop to think about it when we are happy or excited, but when we are down it feels as if we can focus on nothing else but our feelings. When we are down it is as if all the light in the world is gone and will never come back. Life seems to become meaningless and we wonder how we will ever go on. When that happens, what do you do?

1. **Recognize there is a cause.** Sometimes it is easy to know why we are depressed—we just broke up with a girlfriend or boyfriend, we had a fight with someone, we lost an election or game, or any of a number of other reasons that would cause us to feel bad. Knowing there is a temporary reason for it can help you also know that it will pass. Yet sometimes we feel down and the reasons are much less obvious. We are just depressed. This is a good time to pray and search your heart and see if there is some unconscious thing that is eating at you. Discovering what that is can help you deal with it.

2. **Work it through.** God gave us emotions which act as indicators in our lives. Feeling down can be an indicator that it is time to take a break and solve a problem. Ignoring it will not

make it go away. Pray, find out what is wrong, and decide what to do about it.

3. **Talk it out.** Parents and friends can be a great help when you are feeling down. They can also help you work realistically through whatever is bothering you by helping you see things more clearly. Just having the company is often a big help all by itself.

WHEN DO YOU NEED TO GET HELP ABOUT FEELING DOWN?
(When your goose dies?)

Sometimes feeling down is more than it seems, and sometimes it is more than we can handle alone. How do we tell the difference between when we just feel down and when we should get more serious help with being depressed?

In our increasingly disconnected and stressful society, clinical depression is on the rise. This is not just the normal reaction to losing something or someone that causes grief and makes us feel down, but a more general condition that has been recognized by psychologists as being more deeply buried in us and thus more difficult to relieve. It can also have serious side effects and cause health problems.

It can be triggered by an event or simply come about slowly, with no apparent reason at all. A person goes into a state where their mood is continually down. They are constantly sad and may even cry easily and often. Their appetite may change—they may suddenly have no appetite or start eating all of the time. They have no interest in life. In fact, current statistics show that about 4 percent of teenagers get seriously depressed every year.

If you are experiencing these symptoms and just can't seem to shake them for weeks, then perhaps you should talk to someone

SELF-ESTEEM

more seriously about it—someone such as your parents, a church leader, or a school counselor who can refer you to medical help before it becomes a medical problem for you.

Depression is no laughing matter. Getting help as soon as possible is important. If you or a friend are going through a depression that is beginning to affect other areas, it is definitely time to ask for more serious help.

THINK TWICE

No one can make you feel inferior without your consent.

ELEANOR ROOSEVELT

*Nothing is certain in life, but generally the chances
of happiness are greater if one has multiple areas of
interest and involvement. To juggle is to diminish
the risk of depression, anxiety, and unhappiness.*

FAYE J. CROSBY

SOMETHING GOD HAS PROMISED YOU

*God blesses you who weep now,
for the time will come when you will laugh with joy.*

LUKE 6:21 NLT

CONQUERING DEPRESSION

Feeling down often emerges from feeling that you have no control in your own life and are helpless to make things better. In the short term, talking things out with parents and friends and counting your blessings are good ways of pulling yourself out of a slump, but in a longer-term outlook you need to take more control in your life to weaken depression's grip on you. Here are some things you can do to prevent depression from being a common visitor:

- Plan your day. When you set small daily goals, and accomplish them regularly, you feel more in control of your life.
- Have fun regularly. *(Opening my eye was fun!)*
- Stay active. *(Open both eyes!)* Jog, bicycle, play on a sports team, etc.
- Get enough sleep, but also don't sleep too late on the weekends. Get up and get going!
- Avoid junk food and eat nutritiously.
- Don't bury your emotions. Cry if you need to. Express your anger in a healthy way. Talk things out.
- Don't accept negative thoughts or comments from yourself without challenging them. Is what you are saying really true or are you just frustrated?
- Focus on the positive rather than the negative and what you can do rather than what you can't.
- Surround yourself with supportive, encouraging, and uplifting people you can relate to.

DEALING WITH FEELING DOWN

Have You Felt Like Giving Up Lately; A Source Book for Healing Your Hurts by Dave Wilkerson (Fleming Revell, 1980)

DAVID'S DEPRESSION

It must have felt something like having scored the winning touchdown in the state football championship, getting on the honor roll, being elected student body president, and then getting expelled for it. David had slain Goliath, been welcomed into the king's palace, become best friends with the prince, and then he was suddenly on the run for his life. Imagine how you would have felt.

David had times of deep depression. We know this, because we can read about it in the Psalms. He was living in caves, on the run constantly to stay alive, and he had done nothing to deserve it. Another man's jealousy was the root of all of his problems.

Yet rather than dwelling in self-pity, David poured out his heart to God through the songs and prayers that are now recorded in the book of Psalms. He didn't hide his emotions within himself, but he let them loose and turned them over to God. This not only helped him, but it became the songbook of Israel so that others could find comfort in God as well.

I wonder if this is why he was called a man after God's own heart. (See Acts 13:22.)

WORKING THROUGH DEPRESSION

Humble yourselves, therefore, under God's mighty hand,
that he may lift you up in due time. Cast all your
anxiety on him because he cares for you.

1 PETER 5:6-7

There is no perfect solution to depression, nor
should there be. And odd as this may sound . . .
we should be glad of that. It keeps us human.

LESLEY HAZELTON

KICK IT IN GEAR

Name some things that you can do to make yourself better when you feel down. *(Hmmm . . . Hug my dog? Oh, I forgot! I don't have one!)*

1. _____

2. _____

3. _____

4. _____

THE MAIN THING

FEELING DOWN
SOMETIMES IS NORMAL;
BUT DON'T LET IT TAKE
OVER YOUR LIFE!

BEING YOUR OWN BEST FRIEND

(Who better?!)

Do you enjoy your own company? *(Me chill with me?)* People who enjoy spending time alone doing the things they like to do are enjoying their own company. And the funny thing is that often people who enjoy their own company are the same people others enjoy being with. One of the keys to overcoming loneliness is to learn to enjoy your own company.

What do you like to do? What would you like to learn how to do? The answers to these questions are doors into hours of enjoyable time. Do you like to cook? Make a date with yourself to try a new recipe. *(Would I go out with me?)* Subscribe to a couple of cooking magazines. Go to the library and spend an afternoon perusing the many cookbooks for recipes. The next thing you know, you may find yourself in some interesting conversations with avid cooks. And people will always be your friend if you feed them!

Do you like to bicycle? Arrange a weekly bike ride to someplace different each week. Take your camera. Record your impressions of that week's ride in a journal and add photos. Subscribe to a bicycling magazine and read about the bicycle tours available all over the country. Save up and go on an adventure. Maybe a friend would like to go with you. There are bike clubs that sponsor rides on a weekly basis in many cities. Joining them will have you sharing bicycling adventure stories with other enthusiasts in no time.

Eventually any interest pursued faithfully will connect you to others who share that interest, and the next thing you know you will be so busy with your new friendships that you will have to look hard for time alone.

 THINK TWICE

You aren't an accident. (I've caused a few!)
You weren't mass-produced. You aren't an
assembly-line product. You were deliberately
planned, specifically gifted, and lovingly positioned
on this earth by the Master Craftsman.

MAX LUCADO

Until you value yourself you will not value your time.
Until you value your time, you will not do anything with it.

M. SCOTT PECK

SOMETHING GOD HAS PROMISED YOU

O Lord, you have searched me and you know me.

For you created my inmost being; you knit
me together in my mother's womb.

I . . . am fearfully and wonderfully made.

All the days ordained for me were written in
your book before one of them came to be.

PSALM 139:1,13-14,16

GLADYS AYLWARD

Gladys Aylward had two sorrows while growing up: one was that while all her friends had beautiful golden hair, "Mine was black." Her other sorrow? "When all my friends were still growing, I stopped."

When Gladys became a Christian, she had a burning desire to serve the Chinese people, a desire that led her away from England to China.

In China, Gladys ran an inn in which the main entertainment at night was Bible stories. After guests left, they told their friends—spreading the Gospel throughout China. Gladys also took in orphans who were among the many children she found abandoned. During World War II she escaped with one hundred orphans across the country, successfully evading the Japanese invaders. A movie entitled *The Inn of the Sixth Happiness,* starring Ingrid Bergman, tells the story.

Upon arriving in China, the first thing Gladys noticed was that the people of China had black hair—like hers. The second thing she noticed was that all of them "had stopped growing when I did." For the first time, she realized that God had placed the two things she didn't like about herself into her life on purpose, and they were very important to the work she had to do. She said, later, "The Lord God knows what He's doing."

PUT YOUR ZZZ MIND AT REST

"The Ugly Duckling" is not just a story. *(It's a real duck?)* The duckling's quest and happy ending is a pattern that most of us find true to life. If you follow your interests and became the person you were made to be, you will find yourself standing among others like yourself, who have arrived at the swan stage. And you will understand your value and your identity. Don't give up on being you.

KICK IT IN GEAR

List some things you really like to do, even if no one is around. *(Rub mud on my belly?)*

1. _____

2. _____

3. _____

List something below that you would like to learn how to do.

_____

_____

WANT TO GET VERY GOOD AT BEING YOURSELF IN YOUR CAREER CHOICE? TRY THESE SOURCES!

Do What You Love, The Money Will Follow by Marsha Sinetar (DPT, 1989)

What Color Is Your Parachute? 2003 by Richard Nelson Bolles (10 Speed Press, 2002)

THE MAIN THING

IF YOU FOCUS ON YOUR INTERESTS AND NATURAL ABILITIES, YOU WILL FIND YOURSELF SURROUNDED BY FRIENDS.

SELF-ESTEEM

HOW GOD SEES YOU

When God looks at you, what do you think He sees?

Too many people think that God is sitting in heaven waiting for them to mess up so that He can bop them on the head with a stick or something. They think that God, who is perfect, has a hard time dealing with our imperfections. It's as if He is the gym coach who just can't get us to swing the bat right, or the math teacher who throws up their hands when we fail for the twenty-seventh time to balance an equation properly. We get the impression that when He looks down on us He must just shake his head, turn to the angels, and say, "See? What a mess! I don't think they will ever get it! This kid is totally hopeless!"

Yet when we look at the Bible, we get a very different picture of what God sees in us. If we have gone to Him, asked His forgiveness, and made Jesus the Lord of our lives, then the Bible tells us in Psalm 103:12 that He has removed our sins from us as far as the East is from the West. Not only does He separate us from them, but He will never bring them up again. As Corrie Ten Boom said, "When God forgives, He forgets. He buries our sins in the sea and puts a sign on the bank saying, 'No Fishing Allowed.'"

Not only does He forgive us, but when He looks at us, He sees us through Jesus. The Bible phrase for this is "in Christ." In other words, when God looks at a Christian, He sees that person in their relationship to Jesus. If you look through the Bible and see who it says you are "in Christ" it will definitely change your perspective on how you believe God sees you!

Certainly we have some room to grow, but God is rooting *for* us, not *against* us. Sometimes He does correct us to bring us to the point where we will ask His forgiveness, but He does it as a loving Father, not a drill sergeant. God is not as interested in punishing us as He is in bringing us closer to Him.

HOW MUCH DOES GOD THINK YOU ARE WORTH?

How do you judge what something is worth?

Auctioneers and experts in the field travel the country estimating how much something is worth, but none of that really matters once the auction begins. Why? Because they are only estimates.

How is the real value of an item determined? *By what someone is willing to pay for it.*

Using that standard, you are worth a lot more than you probably think, because God paid the ultimate price for you—*His Son.*

As John 3:16 says, "For God so loved the world that he gave his one and only Son, that whoever believes in him shall not perish but have eternal life."

Think about it for a moment. Have you heard that even if you were the only one on earth, God still would have sent His Son to die just for you. That is true. So if that is the case, how much does God think you are worth?

If God sees you as being worth this much, maybe it is time to stop feeling sorry for ourselves and start seeing ourselves the way God sees us. God doesn't make—or pay incredible prices for—any junk!

When we realize how much God values us, it definitely calls for a change in the way we see ourselves. If God values us so much, how can we let anyone else look down on us? Or how can we even look down on ourselves?

💭 THINK TWICE

In the eyes of God, the infinite spirit, all the millions that have lived and now live do not make a crowd, He only sees each individual.

SOREN KIERKEGAARD

Be absolutely certain that our Lord loves you, devotedly and individually, loves you just as you are. . . . Accustom yourself to the wonderful thought that God loves you with a tenderness, a generosity, and an intimacy that surpasses all your dreams.

ABBE HENRI DE TOURVILLE

SOMETHING GOD HAS PROMISED YOU

Before I shaped you in the womb, I knew all about you. Before you saw the light of day, I had holy plans for you.

JEREMIAH 1:5 THE MESSAGE

HOW GOD SEES US: IN JESUS

According to the Bible, when we are in Jesus, the following list of words describes how God sees us:

- Having peace (See John 16:33)

- Justified (See Romans 3:24)
- Not condemned (See Romans 8:1)
- Free from the control of sin and death (See Romans 8:2)
- Safe in the love of God (See Romans 8:38-39)
- Belonging to each other (See Romans 12:5)
- Called to be a saint (See 1 Corinthians 1:2)
- Wise, righteous, sanctified, and redeemed (See 1 Corinthians 1:30)
- Triumphant (See 2 Corinthians 2:14)
- A new creature (See 2 Corinthians 5:17)
- Reconciled with God (See 2 Corinthians 5:19)
- Free (See Galatians 2:4)
- Children of God (See Galatians 3:26)
- Blessed with spiritual blessings (See Ephesians 1:3)
- His workmanship (See Ephesians 2:10)
- Brought close to God (See Ephesians 2:13)
- Sharers together in His promise (See Ephesians 3:6)
- Called with a holy calling (See 2 Timothy 1:9)
- Full of good things (See Philemon 8)

HELPFUL BOOKS

See Yourself As God Sees You by Josh McDowell (Tyndale House Publishers, 1999)

WHEN WE MESS UP

We all mess up. We feel guilty and feel like our friends, our parents, our brother or sister—or even God—probably never wants to see us again. We just want to be alone and get away from it all. But the truth is that never seems to work. *(No matter where I go, there I am!)*

When we mess up, there is no way we can hide it. Sure, sometimes we can escape getting caught, but that doesn't clear things with God. He still knows. Running away from Him is not going to make it better.

First John 1:9 tells us, "If we confess our sins, he [God] is faithful and just and will forgive us our sins and purify us from all unrighteousness." That means if we mess up and turn back to Him, He will give us another chance. Philippians 1:6 says it this way: "He [God] who began a good work in you will carry it on to completion until the day of Christ Jesus."

It is not that sin is not a big deal—if it weren't, there wouldn't have been any need for the cross. But God loves you and wants the best for you so much that He found a way—through the cross—to push sin aside so that He can still have a relationship with you.

If you sin, don't run *from* God—run *to* Him. Ask His forgiveness and don't turn your back on Him. Then live the adventure He has for you—you will never be happy doing anything else.

PUT YOUR 💤 MIND AT REST

Everyone who calls on the name of Jesus will be saved. (See Acts 2:21)

⬆ GETTING GOD INVOLVED

Talk to God about how you feel about yourself and how He sees you. Then sit for a while and listen. Write down anything that He brings to your mind at this time.

1. _____

2. _____

3. _____

Now take a minute to pray about these. If you are unsure how to pray, you can use the prayer below or make up one of your own.

Father, Help me to see myself as You see me and live my life as an ambassador for You. Help me to love others with Your love—as Jesus loved the world—and fulfill Your purpose for me on the earth. I want to fit into Your plans and live out Your plans for my life. Thank You, Lord, for guiding me in these things. Amen

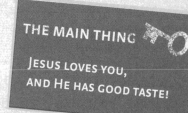

THE MAIN THING

JESUS LOVES YOU, AND HE HAS GOOD TASTE!

THE_GOD IDEA AND CHURCH

We were not designed to go through life alone.

In the first place, God designed us to have fellowship with Him. He wants to help us and guide us into all we can be and to be loved by us just as He loves us. Though He is not physically present with us, He still communicates to us through our consciences and our hearts to lead us every day, if we are willing to listen. God never planned for us to live without Him.

In the second place, God designed us to have fellowship with one another. He put us into families where parents who have lived through all of our struggles before can be constant guides as we grow up. He also gave us a network of extended family members to act as a safety net to help us know our place in the world. Even more He designed the church so that we all can come together and support each other as we strive to be more like Jesus.

God's plan for the church was that the variety of people He created would come together to help build up one another in the love of God. He knows that we are different and have different cultures, backgrounds, hopes, and dreams, but He also planned that by bringing all of those differences together, it would make all of us better for knowing each other. Paul described it this way: "Under his [Jesus'] direction, the whole body [the church] is fitted together perfectly. As each part does its own special work, it helps the other parts grow, so that the whole body is healthy and growing and full of love" (Ephesians 4:16 NLT).

God designed us all to grow up together into all He has planned for us to be. We need each other. *(See? You need me!)*

FINDING YOUR PART IN THE BODY

In various places in the Bible, Paul uses the human body as an illustration of the church. He tells us that God gave us church leaders and ministers to help all of us grow up into the fullness of all that God wants us to be, but also that there is a responsibility for the church members to be ministers to one another and their community. As he said in Ephesians, the responsibility of church leaders and ministers "is to equip God's people to do his [God's] work and build up the church, the body of Christ, until we come to such unity in our faith and knowledge of God's Son that we will be mature and full grown in the Lord, measuring up to the full stature of Christ" (Ephesians 4:12-13 NLT).

In Corinthians he tells us that just as the body has many different parts with different functions, so does the church. It wouldn't be any better for the entire body to be an eye than it would for every member of the church to be the pastor! He also said that just as there are parts of the body that are seen and recognized, like the hands or the nose, there are parts that are covered and are not so obvious, like your heart and your stomach. *(Like, "Hi, I am a liver in the body of Christ!")* Though these things are not visible, they are still crucial to the overall survival of the body.

So guess what? You have a part in all of this too! If you are a member in your church, then God has a part for you to play in making the church a better place. You may want to work setting up the equipment for those who lead worship, or work with the toddlers, help in the office, or whatever. But because you are there doing those things, the church will be a better place because of your efforts!

So find a place to help out. It may seem like work before you start, but you will be blessed as you become a blessing. That is just the way God set it up!

THINK TWICE

It takes both God's power and our effort to produce a loving Christian community. . . . Community is built not on convenience ("We'll get together when I feel like it.") but on the conviction that I need it for spiritual health.

RICK WARREN

The sociability of religion is part of its fundamental nature. The life of religion is always the life of a church.

ROBIN GEORGE COLLINGWOOD

SOMETHING GOD HAS PROMISED YOU

The way God designed our bodies is a model for understanding our lives together as a church: every part dependent on every other part. . . .
You are Christ's body—that's who you are! You must never forget this. Only as you accept your part of that body does your "part" mean anything.

1 CORINTHIANS 12:25, 27 THE MESSAGE

GETTING GOD'S BEAT

Todd always loved music. When he was in middle school he never went anywhere without his CD player and he joined the band as a drummer. For three straight years at Christmas he told his parents that he wanted a drum set, but when the family couldn't find a way for him to practice without driving everyone else crazy, they bought him a guitar. He soon got to the point that he was fiddling around with it more than he watched TV!

About this same time, the church started a band to lead worship for the youth group. Todd was immediately interested, but since he still wasn't very good on the guitar, he started by helping them set up the microphones, running wires, and learning how to work the soundboard. Before too long he was also helping to do the same for the regular services. The youth minister would also let him come in and practice on the band's drum set after school.

By the time Todd was a junior, he was playing drums for the youth group worship band and playing a backup guitar in the church services. As he played and sang, he found music was a great way to express his feelings towards God and all He had done for him.

Now Todd encourages all of his friends to find a place to work in the church. He is also working with musicians from a couple of other local churches to do a musical outreach this summer in the park. He tells everyone that finding his place in the body has made all the difference in the world to how close he is to Jesus.

WANT TO UNDERSTAND MORE OF THE PURPOSE OF THE CHURCH?

The Purpose-Driven Church by Rick Warren (Zondervan, 1995)

An Unstoppable Force: Daring to Become the Church God Had in Mind by Erwin Raphael McManus (Group Publishing Inc, 2001)

GROWING CLOSER TO GOD TOGETHER

Going to church or Bible studies is sometimes the last thing we want to do in our busy lives. When we have to balance that with club meetings, practices, and homework, it can seem pretty low on our list of priorities. However, if we want to be successful at all of those other things, then it may in fact be the most important thing that we do each week.

Our walk with God should touch every area of our lives. If we have parts of ourselves that are shut off to Him, then they may be more of a stumbling block in the end than something which helps us build a solid future. We have to encourage one another and hold each other accountable so that we can grow into the fullness of what God has planned for us.

But you can't do that if your church or Bible study group is more of a social gathering than a family, or is something you attend only when you are not busy with something else. If you don't go to these meetings with the purpose of growing closer to Jesus and the other members of the group each time you meet, then it is not what God intended it to be, but only another social club.

To be real with God, you have to be real with others in your church whether you are in the church building, at school, or doing something together just for fun. So take church seriously—and have fun growing! *(I'm very serious about fun!)*

BELIEVER UNIFYING WORDS

*Let us not give up meeting together, as some are in
the habit of doing, but let us encourage one another—
and all the more as you see the Day approaching.*

HEBREWS 10:25

The Bible knows nothing of solitary religion.

JOHN WESLEY

KICK IT IN GEAR

Here are some areas you might consider working in at
your church. Name a few of your own ideas at the end of
the list.

1. Nursery care
2. Sound equipment
3. Praise and Worship band
4. Choir
5. _____
6. _____

THE MAIN THING

As Christians,
we all need each
others help
to fulfill our
God-given dreams.

SPIRITUAL HEALTH

BREAKING THE AGE BARRIER— FINDING YOUR BARNABAS

When Jesus left, He didn't tell His followers to just go out and make Christians, but to go out and make disciples of the nations. (See Matthew 28:19.)

A disciple is a student who follows his teacher in order to learn how to live. The teacher then not only passes along information, but also leads by example. Today we usually call such teachers *mentors*.

Soon after Saul had become a Christian, Barnabas went to him and took Saul to Antioch to help Barnabas teach and also so Saul could learn more about following Jesus. When Saul went to Jerusalem the first time, most of the people there were afraid to meet with him because of his former reputation as a persecutor of Christians. However, Barnabas intervened, spoke up for Saul, and united him with the other Christians there. Then, as God called them to go out on missionary journeys and take the Gospel to new places, Barnabas also gladly took the backseat as God placed Saul in the forefront and changed his name to Paul. If it had not been for Barnabas' mentoring and championing of Paul, he may never have become the great man of God that we know him as today.

Paul also seemed to have learned the pattern well from Barnabas, as years later he mentored younger men such as Timothy and Titus in how to follow God's calling in their lives. *(Maybe I need that!)*

As young Christians ourselves, we can learn a great deal from those who have traveled the road before us. What we learn from such men and women of God can put us a lot further down the road to fulfilling God's call on our lives than if we just go it alone.

 THINK TWICE

Don't wait for someone to take you under their wing; find a good wing and climb up underneath it.

FRANK C. BUCARO

God never meant us to be wandering around clueless. If you feel that you are wandering, begin praying for a Barnabas to help you find your way. And don't forget to return the favor by being a Barnabas to someone else.

MARIAH THUSICK

SOMETHING GOD HAS PROMISED YOU

Then Barnabas went to Tarsus to look for Saul, and when he found him, he brought him to Antioch. So for a whole year Barnabas and Saul met with the church and taught great numbers of people. The disciples were called Christians first at Antioch.

ACTS 11:25-26

Follow my example, as I follow the example of Christ.

1 CORINTHIANS 11:1

WHAT TO LOOK FOR IN A MENTOR

↳ A mentor should be someone you respect and want to be like, not just someone who is older. If you haven't known them a long time or feel uncomfortable with them, then you should look for someone else to mentor you.

↳ Mentors are people—they aren't perfect. They are bound to make mistakes. As you get to know them, see them for their heart after God, not for any mistakes or personality differences you see along the way.

↳ Mentoring can be formal or informal. You may have people you look up to and want to be like, such as a teacher, minister, or your parents or you may have someone you meet regularly to pray with and grow in the Word.

↳ Sometimes the best way to find a mentor is to find an author or two whom you really respect and read everything they have written. It is not a formal mentoring relationship, but it is a great way to learn more than you can on your own or even from most people in your community.

OTHER THINGS TO CONSIDER WHEN LOOKING FOR A MENTOR

Connecting: The Mentoring Relationships You Need to Succeed by J. Robert Clinton and Paul D. Stanley (Navpress, 1992)

Mentoring: Confidence in Finding a Mentor & Becoming One by Bobb Biehl (Broadman & Holman Publishers, 1997)

PUT YOUR (ZZZ) MIND AT REST

Let God bring the right person to you to mentor you. Don't try to force it yourself.

KICK IT IN GEAR

List some things you have questions about or feel weak in that you think another person might be able to help you with.

1. _____

2. _____

3. _____

List some people you know who are knowledgeable in those fields and might be able to mentor you

1. _____

2. _____

3. _____

THE MAIN THING

OTHERS HAVE WALKED A SIMILAR PATH BEFORE YOU—FOLLOWING THEIR MAPS WILL MAKE THE ROAD EASIER FOR YOU.

MAKE THE BIBLE TALK TO YOU

What would you do if your best friend wrote you a letter and on the outside of the envelope told you that there was some really important information inside it? You rip it open and find several pages—all written in code! Would you then just toss it aside because it is too hard to read, or would you start right away trying to find the key to the code? *(I'd find a new friend!)*

If it were important enough to you, you'd find a way to read the letter, wouldn't you?

Well, guess what? Your Best Friend has written you letters and they are filled with all of the information that you need to know Him better and be a success in your life. All you have to do is read and understand them. Yes, that is right. Jesus' letters to you are all collected in the Bible.

No, the Bible is not in code, but when you first pick it up it can sometimes seem as if it is. Despite the fact that there are lots of different translations of it to help you understand it, it can still be difficult. Yet if you do apply yourself, you can "crack the Bible code" and start learning all the great things this God has locked up in there for you to discover. It just takes a little persistence and determination to get into it. And when you find your first nugget of truth in His letters to you, it feels like He put it there just for you, and you will start to wonder how you survived at all without it!

So roll up your sleeves and get ready to dig in. This section will also give you some tips on how to start "cracking the Bible code" and how to let the Bible speak to you. Get together with your friends and talk about what you are discovering. It is amazing what happens when we start to read the Bible for ourselves. It lets God speak to us in whole new ways!

CRACKING THE COVER TO START FINDING THE SECRETS

Here are some things you can do to start a personal Bible study for yourself that will get you the answers you want from God's Word:

- **Start with the book of John or one of the other gospels.** Since Jesus is the center of the Bible, it is good to start with a book that focuses on Him. John is perhaps the best book of the Bible for learning about Jesus' life and who He was.

- **Take your time, but if you find long lists of names or such, feel free to skim them rather than reading them one by one.** Don't feel like you have to read ten chapters a night or something. In fact, it might be good not to have any set amount of chapters to read each night. Read it as you would a novel and just pick it up sometime during each day and read as much or as little as you like. Think about what you have read.

- **Keep a journal.** Writing down your thoughts about what you have read can really help you get more out of it. Sometimes it is good to ask yourself three basic questions for each section you read: 1) What is being said and who is it being said to? 2) What is the message of this passage? and 3) How can you apply that message to your life?

- **Make a list of things or words in the Bible you have always wondered about and start by studying those.** There are a lot of questions people have about the Bible that don't really help us become better Christians *(You mean like, "Did Adam have a belly button?")*, but there are others that can reveal a great deal to us, like "What does *love* really mean?" Once you have a list of good questions, going to Bible concordances or dictionaries such as *Strong's* and *Vine's* (See page 225 for more information on these two books.) can give you a lot more insight into what is really being said in the verses you are looking at. You can also use them to find out where else in the Bible the same word or words were also used.

THINK TWICE

A thorough knowledge of the Bible is worth more than a college education. (Cheaper too!)

THEODORE ROOSEVELT

The book to read is not the one which thinks for you, but the one which makes you think. No book in the world equals the Bible for that.

MCCOSH

SOMETHING GOD HAS PROMISED YOU

You have received the Holy Spirit, and he lives within you, so you don't need anyone to teach you what is true. For the Spirit teaches you all things, and what he teaches is true—it is not a lie. So continue in what he has taught you, and continue to live in Christ.

1 JOHN 2:27 NLT

The main thing to keep in mind here is that no prophecy of Scripture is a matter of private opinion. And why? Because it's not something concocted in the human heart. Prophecy resulted when the Holy Spirit prompted men and women to speak God's Word.

2 PETER 1:20-21 THE MESSAGE

SOME BASIC RULES FOR UNDERSTANDING THE BIBLE

↳ Remembering some of the following guidelines can help you to keep from misunderstanding passages of the Bible:

↳ Pray that God will help you understand what you are reading before you begin.

↳ Who is speaking? Is it God, Jesus, a demon, an angel, or a man?

↳ Who is the passage addressing? It is written to the nation of Israel, unbelievers, the church, or some other group or individual?

↳ What is going on or being said in the passages surrounding the verses you are reading? Sometimes a scripture can seem to be very different when taken alone rather than when taken in relationship to what the entire passage or chapter is discussing.

↳ What is your common sense understanding of the passage? Don't overanalyze. Let the Bible speak to you as if Jesus were there speaking it to you in person.

ONLINE BIBLE STUDY HELP

www.biblegateway.com

www.gospelcom.net

HELPFUL B👓KS

How to Study Your Bible for Teens by Kay Arthur, BJ Lawson, and David Lawson (Harvest House Publishers, Inc, 2003)

The New Strong's Exhaustive Concordance of the Bible by James Strong (Thomas Nelson Publishers, 1996)

Vine's Complete Expository Dictionary of Old and New Testament Words by W. E. Vine (Thomas Nelson Publishers, 1996)

OVERCOMING OBSTACLES

List the things you think will slow you down. *Example:*

OBSTACLE: Whenever I start reading the Bible, I always fall asleep.

POSSIBLE SOLUTIONS: Maybe I could read it in the morning rather than right before I go to bed at night or read it at the kitchen table rather than in my room. Maybe I could also get it on tape or CD and listen to it as I am getting ready for school in the morning, straightening up my room, or things like that. *(Or I could read standing on my head!)*

OBSTACLE

_____

_____

POSSIBLE SOLUTIONS:

_____

_____

_____

OBSTACLE

_____

_____

POSSIBLE SOLUTIONS:

_____

_____

_____

PUT YOUR  MIND AT REST

God gave us the Holy Spirit to help us learn everything that we need to know. (See John 16:13)

⬆ GETTING GOD INVOLVED

Talk to God about reading His Word and ask for His wisdom and help. Then sit for a while and listen. Write down anything that He brings to your mind at this time.

1. _____

2. _____

3. _____

Now take a minute to pray about these. If you are unsure how to pray, you can use the prayer below or make up one of your own.

SPIRITUAL HEALTH

Father, I want to get to know You better and also Your Son, Jesus. I realize that a lot of what I need to know You have put into Your letters to me—the Bible. Help me as I am reading Your Word to understand it and get from it what You want me to get. Teach me and guide me as I read it. Thank You. Amen

THE MAIN THING

STUDYING THE BIBLE HELPS YOU ACCOMPLISH YOUR GOD-GIVEN DREAMS.
(SEE 2 PETER 1:3-4)

CONNECT WITH THAT GOD PERSON YOURSELF

(Who? Me?)

Most of us, if we heard someone say to us, "Well, the other day, God told me . . ." we would probably think that person a little odd, at best. *(More likely completely wacko!)* God doesn't talk to people individually anymore—or does He?

Well, if we really believe what the Bible says, there is no reason why He wouldn't. We find places where God spoke directly to people all the way from Adam to the disciple John in the book of Revelation. He spoke to the prophet Samuel when he was a child, to Paul when he was still God's enemy, and to the crowd who saw Jesus baptized. God hasn't changed—there is no reason why He can't still talk to people audibly today just as He did in Bible days.

However, connecting with God today is more of a heart issue than a telephone call. As we draw nearer to God, it is through our consciences that He usually speaks to us. So how do we get to the point of telling whether it is God speaking to our hearts or just our own thoughts in our heads? *(My head is noisy!)*

The Bible tells us that the sheep know the Shepherd's voice. (See John 10:4.) That is because they are with the Shepherd all of the time and are used to his voice. Have you ever been in a crowded room full of people chattering and then suddenly heard your mom or dad's voice mixed in with the rest? Somehow, despite the confusion, you "locked on to their signal" and heard only them. It is a lot like that with God as well. As you learn to follow in the way that He leads you, it will get easier and easier to know when He is speaking to you.

Will God ever speak to you in an audible voice? It is possible, but not something that you can force. What you can do, however, is learn to connect with Him regularly in your heart.

THE FIVE P'S FOR POWER

The Bible tells us that if we will seek God with all of our hearts, then we will find him. (See Jeremiah 29:13.) Here are some habits that you can form to help you grow closer to God day by day:

1. **Praise God regularly.** Don't do this in church only, but also when you are alone with God. Count your blessings and thank God for all the good things that He has done for you. Thank Him for your health, the stability of your family, for good friends, your home, or anything that you are thankful for. When you praise God, it opens your heart for more of His presence in your life and more for His goodness to flow through you.

2. **Pray.** Prayer is simply conversation with God—and conversation is not a monologue, but a dialogue, meaning both people speak, and both people listen. Take time to go over the details of your day with God and pray for friends and loved ones; but also take some time to just listen to what He is saying to you in your heart.

3. **Pore over the Bible.** Take time not only to read your Bible, but also to think about it and ponder what it says. If it is a story imagine what it must have been like for the people who were involved in it. Think about how the teaching applied to the people who heard it, and how it applies to you today.

4. **Put it into Practice.** You will notice that this last habit has two p's in it, because it may be the most important one of all. When you put into practice the things that you have learned from God, incredible things can happen. You also exercise your faith by following God's guidelines for how things should be done rather than just following what the crowd does. It means putting God first in what you do and letting Him have a big part in your daily life. That is where the real power comes from!

 **THINK TWICE**

Knowing God is more than knowing about Him; it is a matter of dealing with Him as He opens up to you, and being dealt with by Him as He takes knowledge of you. Knowing about Him is a necessary precondition of trusting in Him, but the width of our knowledge about Him is no gauge of our knowledge of Him.

JAMES I. PACKER

The Bible is filled with assurances of God's help and comfort in every kind of trouble which might cause fears to arise in the human heart. You can look ahead with promise, hope, and joy.

BILLY GRAHAM

SOMETHING GOD HAS PROMISED YOU

Draw close to God, and God will draw close to you.

JAMES 4:8 NLT

SPIRITUAL HEALTH

WITH ALL HER HEART: CATHERINE BOOTH

Catherine had been a Christian as long as she could remember. She learned to read by reading the Bible and often read it out loud as her mother sewed or worked close by.

Yet, when she was seventeen, this was no longer enough. She wanted to know in her heart that she was saved, not just that she had followed some formula to be religious or was a member of a local church. Within her had grown an intense desire to know God personally.

So she started praying and earnestly seeking God. Some nights she would pray until 2:00 a.m. and then throw herself down on the bed and fall asleep, hoping that the morning would bring the assurance that she was seeking. She kept this up for six weeks, never finding what she was after, but still believing that in the end she would.

Then, on the morning of June 15, 1846, she awoke after another late night of such prayer, and as her eyes fell on a verse in one of her hymnals, the assurance she had been seeking filled her heart. It was as if Jesus had walked into the room and touched her! She had the answer to her prayers.

She later married William Booth and together they founded the Salvation Army, which not only helped the poor as it still does today, but became one of the most vibrant missionary outreaches the world had ever seen. Being determined to know God personally and not just know *about* Him set the groundwork in her heart for her to be used powerfully by God.

WANT TO GET TO KNOW GOD PERSONALLY?

Experiencing God: Knowing and Doing His Will by Henry T. Blackaby (Broadman & Holman Publishers, 1998)

Celebration of Discipline: The Path to Spiritual Growth by Richard J. Foster (Harper San Francisco, 2003)

DO YOU REALLY WANT TO KNOW GOD?

In the modern world that we live in, if we don't get satisfaction from something pretty quickly, we often get bored and abandon it. Yet some things that are really worth doing take a lot of time, like learning to play a sport well, reading a good book, learning to play an instrument, getting enough money to buy a car from working summer jobs, as well as a lot of other things. Yet even in these pursuits, if we don't find a little success along the way every so often, we find something else to do.

However, many great pursuits happen only when you stick to things for a long time without any appearance of success. Thomas Edison, for example, failed over 2,000 times before he found the right filament to light a light bulb. How long do you think you would have stuck to it before you quit? Would you have gone the distance?

The experience of finding God can seem the same way. It is a pursuit that can even seem to be hopeless. Some people look for Him for a little while and then quit in disappointment, throw up their hands, and think He can no longer be found today like He was in Bible times. Yet we see too many examples in our own times of those who have found Him for that to be true. The difference is that those who find Him really want to find Him and refuse to quit until they do—even if it takes their entire lifetimes to do so!

WHAT PRAYER DOES

Call to me and I will answer you. I'll tell you marvelous and wondrous things that you could never figure out on your own.

JEREMIAH 33:3 THE MESSAGE

Prayer enlarges the heart until it is capable of containing God's gift of himself.

MOTHER TERESA

KICK IT IN GEAR

Write some questions you would like to have God answer for you either through your Bible reading or through talking to you as you pray. Put a date beside each question as you receive His answers.

1. _____

2. _____

3. _____

4. _____

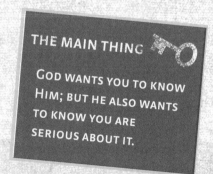

THE MAIN THING

GOD WANTS YOU TO KNOW HIM; BUT HE ALSO WANTS TO KNOW YOU ARE SERIOUS ABOUT IT.

TEACHERS—TEACHER TUNE-UP

IT'S ABOUT INTEGRITY AND CARING

(Like they are people or something. Yeah!)

Teachers can be tough. Sometimes the best ones are the toughest. Yet it is one thing for a teacher to challenge you or move you towards your best and quite another if they won't help when you just don't get it! If you find yourself frustrated with a teacher, here are some things to try:

1. **Talk with them on your own and get their perspective.** What is it that you are doing or not doing that is affecting your relationship with this teacher or your grade in their class? Are you simply misunderstanding things or missing assignments, or are you just not understanding some basic concepts that you should have mastered by now? Or maybe they just made a mistake.

2. **If you have a hard time relating with that teacher, talk with another teacher that you have had before who teaches the same subject and see if they can help.** Believe it or not, teachers become friends with one another. They have often worked successfully with the teacher you are having issues with, so they will probably have some insights into how you can work with them successfully as well. Try getting advice from someone else who has been in their class before. That also might work.

3. **Do what you say you are going to do and get your work done well and on time.** If you have done everything you are supposed to have done, then oftentimes there will be no more room for problems. The teacher may still be strict, but if you meet their challenge, then it will be easier to handle.

Yes, teachers are people too. Usually if they can count on you do to what is right, you can count on them to do the same.

WHAT IF WE JUST DON'T GET ALONG?

Have you ever noticed with some people that you just don't click? Their jokes aren't funny, they always say things that rub you the wrong way, and if you have a choice, you would rather be as far from them as possible? Well, believe it or not, that is pretty normal. With all of the different personality types in our world, not all of them are ones that we can just naturally "click with." Now that doesn't let us off the hook from "loving our neighbor as ourselves," but it doesn't mean that we have to go against the grain to be best friends with them either. We can let them have their space and still not make fun of them or put them down because they are different. We can "live and let live," as the old saying goes.

However, this is not so easy when the person who grates on us is a teacher! If every day you go to their class and their jokes set your teeth on edge and you are just generally bugged throughout their lessons, then you will have a tough time being inspired and performing well in their class. They may actually be great teachers, but you just don't see it. Well, guess what? The grade you get in that class still goes on your report card. How do you make it through something like that?

This is another "welcome to real life" situation. You have to figure it out. People experience the same thing when they go to work and have a boss they don't get along with very well, but they either cope with it or struggle the rest of their lives because they can't overcome their own feelings.

With teachers, it is a bit easier, as you have to see them only one period a day, but you have to reach down inside yourself and love them with God's love. See them as God sees them. If they don't motivate you, you have to motivate yourself. With God's help and the fruit of the Spirit operating in your life, this is all possible. So don't let your attitude stand in the way of your success! Change it and you will be surprised how well you can do!

THINK TWICE

Adversity is the trial of principle. Without it,
a man hardly knows whether he is honest or not.

HENRY FIELDING

One cool judgment is worth a thousand hasty counsels.
The thing to do is to supply light and not heat.

WOODROW WILSON

SOMETHING GOD HAS PROMISED YOU

I urge, then, first of all, that requests, prayers,
intercession and thanksgiving be made for everyone—
for kings and all those in authority, that we may live
peaceful and quiet lives in all godliness and holiness.

1 TIMOTHY 2:1-2

GET ALONG BETTER WITH YOUR TEACHERS BY REMEMBERING THESE THINGS

↳ Just as it says in Timothy, remember to pray for your teachers and others who have authority over you.

↳ Try to honestly see things from the teacher's point of view.

↳ Make sure that your behavior toward your teachers is always respectful and friendly, and they are more likely to be respectful and friendly to you as well.

↳ Don't embarrass your teacher.

↳ Sharpen your listening skills and apply yourself more in their class. *(Sharpen your pencils and apply them also!)*

↳ Ask good, relevant questions in class. A lot of times teachers will take more interest in you if you take more interest in what they are trying to teach you. Plus, class participation is often part of your grade.

↳ If you are still having a problem, ask your questions immediately after class rather than letting it become even more of a problem than it already is.

↳ Teachers have interests besides what they do in the classroom. Perhaps you can find a way to connect centered around one of those interests that you share.

↳ If all else fails, ask for a parent/teacher conference and see if you can be there as well. A lot of times things are easier to work out if your parents are there with you.

↳ Talk with your guidance counselor about the problem. If you can't find a solution, then you might be better off finding another teacher who teaches the same class.

 OVERCOMING OBSTACLES

List the things you are struggling with at school. *Example:*

OBSTACLE: My English teacher grades too strictly.

POSSIBLE SOLUTIONS: I could go and talk to her about it and find out what she expects me to be doing that I am not doing. Or I could take in a particular test or paper that I thought had a grade which was lower than I expected and find out from her what I needed to do to receive a higher grade. I could also ask my friend's sister what I could do, because she had this teacher last year.

OBSTACLE _____

POSSIBLE SOLUTIONS:

_____

_____

OBSTACLE _____

POSSIBLE SOLUTIONS:

_____

_____

PUT YOUR ZZZ MIND AT REST

Teachers are there to get the best out of you. Don't fight them in this, but help them get the best out of you.

⬆ GETTING GOD INVOLVED

Talk to God about your relationships with your teachers and ask for His wisdom and help. Then sit for a while and listen. Write down anything that He brings to your mind at this time.

1. _____

2. _____

3. _____

Now take a minute to pray about these. If you are unsure how to pray, you can use the prayer below or make up one of your own.

Father, Bless my teachers. Help me to understand them more and relate to them better. Give us an opportunity to talk honestly and clearly. Lord, if there is anything that is in their personal life that is causing them pain or stress, please comfort them and help them to solve their problem. Be a light to them, Lord, and touch their lives with Your presence and Your joy. Thank You. Amen

THE MAIN THING

YOU ARE IN SCHOOL TO LEARN AND PREPARE FOR YOUR FUTURE.

TIME MANAGEMENT— GET IT ALL DONE

PROPER PLANNING *(I need three of me!)*

Your family is leaving for a ski retreat in Colorado after school tomorrow and it's the end of the second quarter—you have papers due tomorrow for English and history and that algebra exam to take—so you need to pack, study, and write two papers. There's also that last episode of *Survivor* on TV that you wanted to watch tonight and see who wins. So you just figure you'll stay up all night and do it all. Then you wake up ten minutes before the bell for first period with a puddle of drool on page 57 of your algebra book and realize you haven't even started the first paper. What are you going to do? *(How did I get into this situation—AGAIN!)*

The truth is that those papers were assigned over a month ago and you knew you would have midterm tests coming up. You had plenty of time to get it all done and watch your show—you just didn't! *(Stop! I'm trying to be the victim here!)*

In the book *Seven Habits of Effective People,* *(Oh no, I read the one about defective people!)* Steven Covey gave the following illustration to help us visualize the solution to just this problem: Imagine that the time you have is a jar and you have three sets of objects to fill it—some sand, a bunch of pebbles and medium-sized rocks, and some bigger rocks. If you take the sand and pour it in, then you can pile about half of the pebbles in and the jar is full. No room for the big rocks at all. But if you put the big rocks in first, there is plenty of room to pour in a bunch of the pebbles and most of the sand.

The big rocks are the important things you need to finish: the papers, studying for your tests, and packing for your trip. The medium-sized rocks are the things you like to do for yourself, like watching your TV show. If you put the "big things" into your time jar first, there is plenty of time for the other things; but it doesn't work the other way around. You have to plan your time!

GETTING DOWN TO THE NITTY GRITTY

In a famous Harvard University study, students were asked whether or not they set goals for themselves on a regular basis. Only three percent of them said they did.

Thirty years later, these same students were found again. The most successful members of the group were the three percent who had continued that college habit of setting goals.

The Bible says it this way, *Where there is no vision, the people perish* (Proverbs 29:18 KJV). People who set goals accomplish things!

However, time management speaker Bob Harrison says, "Setting goals is the most dangerous thing a person can do." *(Hang on! Dangerous?)*

The reason is that we often focus our goals on financial and professional success and forget the important things such as family, friends, and health. Setting a goal in one area focuses you on that area, often to the exclusion of all others. When we set our goals, we have to be balanced and make sure that the big rocks we choose to put into our time jars first are truly big rocks.

Having the right priorities is an essential key.

There is another simple rule of time management that has been quoted by so many people it is hard to tell who first said it. It is this: Each night before you go to bed, write down the six most important things you have to do the next day, in their order of importance. Then when you get up the next morning, start at the top of the list and work your way down. Then if you don't finish, carry them over to your list for the next day and continue. You won't believe how much more you will accomplish!

 **TH!NK TWICE**

Far away in the sunshine are my highest aspirations.
I may not reach them, but I can look up and see the
beauty, believe in them, and try to follow where they lead.

LOUISA MAY ALCOTT

We never plan to fail; but we often do when we fail to plan.

ANONYMOUS

(With better planning, "Mr Anonymous" would have gotten credit for this quote!)

SOMETHING GOD HAS PROMISED YOU

Therefore be careful how you walk, not as unwise men
but as wise, making the most of your time.

EPHESIANS 5:15-16 NASB

TAKING ACCOUNT

Ken sat looking at the two pieces of paper in disbelief. A month ago, Sarah, his youth leader at church, had talked about values and given them a little test. He was sure he had passed with flying colors: God first, then family, school, friends, etc.—he had all the right answers and in the right order. Now that same piece of paper was giving him a lump in his throat.

Just last week, Sarah had given them another challenge: to keep track of how they spend their time for one week. Everyone who did it got five dollars. Again he had won the prize! But as he felt the crispness of the new five-dollar bill in his hand, Sarah had them cross out all the time spent doing things they had to do—school, chores, wrestling practice—and then add up how much time they spent doing each of the things that remained. These they were to put in order from greatest to least.

Then she handed back the values test from the month before. "Compare the two lists," she said. "The one list shows the things you say you value, but the other shows the ones you spend your time on, the things you do. Actions speak louder than words. Do your actions show that you really value the things you said you do?"

Ken looked at the lists. They were very different. He'd been fooling himself. The truth was there in black and white—he'd lied to himself. When he prayed at the end of that meeting, he promised God and himself there would be some changes.

WANT TO MANAGE YOUR TIME BETTER?

The One-Minute Manager by Kenneth H. Blanchard and Spencer Johnson (Berkley Pub Group, 1983).

The Seven Habits of Highly Effective People by Stephen R. Covey (Simon & Schuster, 1990).

The Personal Efficiency Program: How to Get Organized to Do More in Less Time by Kerry Gleeson (Wiley & Sons, 1994).

DON'T CONFUSE ACTIVITY WITH ACCOMPLISHMENT

In our modern, microwave, fast-food-paced society, chores, schoolwork, clubs, student counsel, youth group, and/or sports activities seem to clog our schedules and there is little time left to even breathe. We are in constant motion all day, and then rush home to shut our bedroom door to catch up on tomorrow's homework. No one could possibly call us lazy or unmotivated, but in all this ceaseless action, what are we really accomplishing?

In running our lives this way, we often make the same mistake many hamsters do. Hamsters get on those little wheels in their cages and make the wheels spin like crazy, but they never get anywhere. In our frenzy of activities, do we ever stop to think that despite the fact that we are always doing something, we may not be getting anything done that is worth getting done? *(Puff! Puff! I can't think about that right now! I'm too busy!)*

What is it that you really want to accomplish in your life? What is the God-given dream that has been placed in your heart? Are the things you are doing leading you to accomplish that or simply keeping you busy so that you don't notice that your hopes and dreams are getting farther away rather than nearer? It is quite possible that you could accomplish more by doing less.

TIME SAVING WORDS

Careful planning puts you ahead in the long run;
hurry and scurry puts you further behind.

PROVERBS 21:5 THE MESSAGE

Most people are more concerned with doing
things right than doing the right things.

PETER DRUCKER

KICK IT IN GEAR ⚡

List six things you need—or want—to accomplish in the next year.

1. _____
2. _____
3. _____
4. _____
5. _____
6. _____

List the six most important things you will do to start accomplishing these things TODAY.

1. _____
2. _____
3. _____
4. _____
5. _____
6. _____

THE MAIN THING

EVERYONE HAS THE SAME AMOUNT OF TIME . . . SUCCESS IS DETERMINED BY HOW WE USE IT!

TRAVEL—THE SUITCASE AND TRAVEL THING

PACKING THAT BAG

Hear are some quick and easy things to remember when you are packing for a trip:

1. **Find out what the weather will be like where you are going.** Check the extended forecast for the area on a Web site such as www.weather.com for the length of your stay so that you take the appropriate clothing.

2. **Plan your wardrobe.** Take mix-and-match clothing rather than outfits, and figure out if you need to pack anything more formal for special events. The old saying is, "Bring half as many clothes as you think you need and twice as much money." (For a complete suggested list, check out the universal packing list at upl.codeq.info or the one-bag, one-page packing list at www.oratory.com/onebag/what2take.pdf.)

3. **Plan to wash your clothes.** Too many people think that if they are going for seven days, they need seven shirts, seven pairs of pants, seven sets of underwear, etc. *(Hmmm . . .)* Plan to wash clothes every three or four days or even every day—it is easier if you are moving from place to place to wash things in the hotel or B & B sink every night before you go to bed so that they will be clean and dry the next morning. Eliminate anything you aren't sure you will be wearing, except perhaps one outfit for special occasions. *(Excuse me while I empty my bags!)*

4. **Bathroom stuff.** Pack only what you need. Often shampoo, soap, etc. are provided if you are staying in a hotel. If not, get small containers for such things. Most stores have a section that sells travel-sized items.

5. **Pack comfortable shoes only.** *(Your feet will thank you!)* Don't take more than two pairs, and often one pair will do. A good pair of dark casual shoes can be worn for sightseeing or a nice evening out, whereas white tennis or running shoes aren't as versatile. Avoid shoes with metal in the soles because of airport security metal detectors.

6. **Check baggage restrictions before you go.** Most airlines, bus services, and trains have a place on their Web sites that give you the dimension and weight limits for stored baggage and carry-ons. Make sure these are under the limit before you leave—you can save yourself a lot of problems. Also check the return limits—which can be different (especially if traveling abroad), and make sure you also stay within those limits.

7. **Take a sturdy bag that meets your needs and which you can find easily at the airport.** Why do so many people have black bags with rollers? You would be surprised by how difficult it is to identify your luggage at the airport turnstiles, let alone describe it if it gets lost. If you do have a bag that looks like everyone else's, try tying some bright ribbons or a scarf around the handles, and make sure you have tags on it that have both your home address and the address where you are going to be staying on your trip.

8. **Buddy packing.** If you are traveling with a close friend or relative and will be staying together, consider packing half of each other's things in the other person's suitcase. That way if one is

misplaced on the way there, then at least you will have clothing until the airline can find it and get it to you.

9. **Bundle clothes rather than folding them.** Roll smaller clothing inside of larger things. This eliminates creases that would force you to have to iron things when you reach your destination. (For more on this, check out www.oratory.com/onebag/packing.html.)

TH!NK TWICE

I have yet to hear of someone returning from an extended trip who vows to take more stuff the next time!

DOUG DYMENT
Travel Writer

September is, by far, the best month to go just about anywhere.

JOHN FLINN

SOMETHING GOD HAS PROMISED YOU

I am with you always.

MATTHEW 28:20

KICK IT IN GEAR

Getting ready for a trip? Here is a list of things to do to get you on the right track.

1. A month or so before you leave, begin a list of things you want to remember to pack. *(Right shoe, left shoe . . .)*

2. A week before, begin putting things in the suitcase.

3. The day before, close the suitcase and let things settle.

4. The day of your trip, add last-minute items to the spaces opened up by the settling.

NEED MORE HELP PACKING? TRY THESE SOURCES!

Smart Packing for Today's Traveler by Susan Foster (Smart Travel Press, 2000)

Travel and packing tip Web sites

www.onebag.com

www.travelite.org

www.eurotrip.com/preparation_and_packing/index.html

For travel advisories and tips for getting through security www.TSATravelTips.us

THE MAIN THING

TRAVEL LIGHT.

HOW TO BE A GUEST IN SOMEONE'S HOME

One of the greatest opportunities when you travel—whether it is to Europe, somewhere else in the U.S., or the farthest reaches of Africa—is to be able to stay in someone's home who is a native to that area. Sure, sightseeing, reading tour books, and traveling around are great ways to get to know the country, but if you really want to learn how their culture is different from your own, living with a local family is the best way to do it!

When you go, however, remember that their home is a home, not a hotel. Be respectful of their things and the way they live. Keep your own things neat, out of the way, and stowed in your suitcase or space that they have provided for you. Make your own bed every morning and keep your room straightened up. Your presence, except for your smiling self, should be as invisible as possible. *(Invisible man goes visiting.)*

Another important thing to remember is to interact with the family when you are with them, but don't be a nuisance. When you sit down to eat with them, ask questions about the area and about what is unique to it. Ask about their family history and stories. And also be willing to tell them about where you live and about your own culture and family.

The key thing is to, of course, be considerate and be a guest whom they would want to welcome back in case you were ever in the area again. A good way to remember how to act is to think about what it would be like to be their host, and then act accordingly.

So, bon voyage! Any opportunity to be a guest in someone else's home is an adventure. Don't forget to have fun!

OTHER TRAVEL TIPS

Here are some other helpful things that you can do to be a better guest and have a great trip:

1. **Plan your daily schedule before you arrive, but also leave room for changes.** This way, once you arrive, there will be less pressure on your host family to entertain you while you are there. It is a good idea to sit down with them when you arrive, go over your schedule and make changes, if necessary, when they have activities planned for you. This will also let them know where you are going to be most of the time.

2. **Be a courteous traveler.** It is often a lot of fun to pile onto a plane, bus, or train with a group of friends going somewhere new, but after several hours your "enthusiasm" can wear dramatically on the other passengers. Have fun, but don't be rude or inconsiderate while you are on the way to or on the way back from your big adventure.

3. **Pack a good carry-on.** Take a change of clothes, basic bathroom supplies, and things to entertain yourself on the trip. This way if your bags are lost, at least you will have a change of clothes for the next day. *(It is also nice to brush your teeth and comb your hair. You don't want to scare your hosts!)*

4. **Carry your passport, money, and other valuables securely.** Often you can take them in a pouch that goes around your neck and under your shirt or tucks into your pants. This keeps

thieves from getting to them easily and avoids having your host family support you once you get there.

5. **Pack clothing appropriate for the culture where you are going.** For example, shorts are often not appropriate in some cultures for either men or women, *(Some people just can't take knobby knees!)* so find out before you pack if any of your clothing should be exchanged for more appropriate clothing.

 **THINK TWICE**

*This ideal guest is an equally ideal hostess (or host);
the principle of both is the same. A ready smile,
a quick sympathy, a happy outlook, consideration
for others, tenderness toward everything that is
young or helpless, and forgetfulness of self.*

EMILY POST

*If you wish to travel far and fast, travel light. Take off all your
envies, jealousies, unforgiveness, selfishness, and fears.*

GLENN CLARK

SOMETHING GOD HAS PROMISED YOU

When you enter a house, first say, "Peace to this house."

LUKE 10:5

BE A GREAT HOUSEGUEST BY REMEMBERING THIS

↳ When you arrive, take a gift for your hosts. This can be a small thing such as a nice box of chocolates, or if you are staying with someone from another country or culture, give them a gift that is indigenous to where you live.

↳ Don't overstay your welcome.

↳ Receive gifts from your host graciously.

↳ Be respectful of your elders in the home.

↳ Help with chores when you can: clearing and washing dishes, taking out the trash, reading to younger children, etc.

↳ If you are traveling abroad, find out as much as you can about local customs and follow them.

↳ If the family has any unique customs follow those as well.

↳ Remember your manners at all times: say please and thank you, and don't go into parts of the home where you are not invited.

↳ Don't comment in a disapproving manner on the way the people live. You are their guest, not their critic. *(Pretend you don't notice their housgoats!)*

↳ Be prepared to entertain yourself. Take a book or something else to occupy your time. Don't expect them to constantly entertain you.

↳ When they do entertain you, always be a willing participant to go somewhere with them or take part in the activity that they propose.

↳ Thank them when you leave. Another gift would also be appropriate here. And let them know they are always welcome in your home too.

GET YOURSELF IN THE KNOW

Here are some other places you might want to take a look to find out more about where you are traveling:

1. Friends, family, or friends of friends *(or families of friends or families of families? Stop!)*

2. Books from your library
3. Check the travel section of your local bookstore
4. Web sites
5. Tourist bureaus or travel agencies
6. Other sources you can think of

_____

_____

_____

(LOOK HERE TOO!)

Traveler's Tool Kit (3rd Edition) by Rob Sangster (Menasha Ridge Press, 2000)

Emily Post's Etiquette (16th Edition) by Peggy Post (HarperCollins, 1997)

PUT YOUR 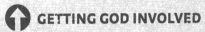 MIND AT REST

Your hosts will be grateful and flattered by any research you do before you go. So every little bit helps!

🔼 GETTING GOD INVOLVED

Talk to God about your trip and ask for His wisdom and help. Then sit for a while and listen. Write down anything that He brings to your mind at this time.

1. _____

2. _____

3. _____

Now take a minute to pray about these. If you are unsure how to pray, you can use the prayer below or make up one of your own.

Father, I ask You that everything during my trips goes well, that You will keep my luggage safe and make sure it arrives with me, and that You will keep me from losing anything or having it stolen. I thank You also that nothing that I eat will make me ill and take away from my experience of a new place.

I also pray that You will help me to be a blessing to the family that I am staying with. Help me to remember how to be the type of guest they would gladly welcome back again. Thank You. Amen

THE MAIN THING

BE A BLESSING AND AN AMBASSADOR FOR GOD WHEREVER YOU GO.

Acknowledgements

[87] Christopher John Farley, "Reborn to Be Wild," *Time*. 22 January 1996. http://www.jarchives.com/vault076.htm

[139] Thomas Stanley and William Danko, *The Millionaire Next Door: The Surprising Secrets of America's Wealthy* (Atlanta: Longstreet Press 1996), 8-11.

[97] Prom estimates taken from ThePromSite.com, www.thepromsite.com, Accessed 3 December, 2003 http://thepromsite.com/budget/index.html

[140-41] Robert Kiyosaki, *Rich Dad, Poor Dad: What the Rich Teach their Kids about Money—that the Poor and the Middle Class do Not!* (Scottsdale: TechPress, Inc., 1997, 1998), 180-2.

[174] Statistics taken from Ncadd.org, www.ncadd.org, Accessed 3 December, 2003 http://www.ncadd.org/facts/numberoneprob.html

Additional copies of this
and other Honor Books products
are available from your local bookstore.

If you have enjoyed this book,
or if it has had an impact on your life,
we would like to hear from you.

Please contact us at:
Cook Communications Ministries, Dept. 201
4050 Lee Vance View
Colorado Springs, CO 80918
Or visit our website: www.cookministries.com

HONOR ℍ BOOKS

Inspiration and Motivation for the Season of Life